DEEP BODYWORK AND PERSONAL DEVELOPMENT

Harmonizing our Bodies, Emotions, and Thoughts

Jack W. Painter

Also available by Jack Painter: TECHNICAL MANUAL OF DEEP WHOLISTIC BODYWORK (Bodymind Books, 450 Hillside Avenue, Mill Valley, CA 94941, Tel. 415-383-4017; write for free brochure).

Other versions of the present volume have been published in French (Le Jour, Montreal), German (Koesel Verlag, Munich), Italian (Sugarco, Milano), Danish (Borgen Vorlag, Copenhagen), and Spanish (Pax-Mexico, Liberia Carlos Cesarmen, Mexico, D.F.)

Bodymind Books, 450 Hillside Avenue, Mill Valley, CA 94941

ISBN 0-938405-01-2

This book is dedicated
to the two loves of my life,

Claire and Isa Lora

TABLE OF CONTENTS

Photographs by Margaret Boyles. Illustrations by Christine Fessler,
Christopher Gouvea, Karin Lynch and Tim Tollefson.

FOREWORD

Those of us who are giving birth to the new field of Somatics have a lot to be thankful for in Jack Painter's work. He has done the incredible labor of producing a textbook of our field. The beauty of this book is multifaceted. It is a concise and crystalline description of the method of deep tissue bodywork. The descriptions of technique read like a manual. That alone is a major accomplishment.

But Jack Painter has done more than document method. He has created a natural synthesis of the theory and philosophy of body- oriented work with descriptions of the work. In doing this he reveals the nuts and bolts of how and why the bodywork is practiced by the bodyworker who is both artist and therapist.

I think this book is a major contribution to Western Psychology, which is just beginning to realize that Somatic teachers have been demonstrating for years: in therapy and education, we must learn from the wisdom of the body. Jack Painter is a pioneer in the development of bodywork, and this book is a wonderful map.

Robert K. Hall, M.D.
Lomi School,
Mill Valley, Ca.

INTRODUCTION

Jack's an old friend of mine. Writing the introduction to one of his books seems a grand opportunity to reminisce a little, while saying a few things about the book too. Two themes come quickly to mind. In the first Jack is in his home in Mill Valley, sitting on a wooden chair in the middle of his large spacious living room with a music stand in front of him, encircled by fake books of sheet music, playing his flugelhorn just for himself. Here's a guy who knows how to take time out. He knows how to let the rest of the world go by for a while, while he refuels. I always associated that scene with Jack's keen sense of living from his center. He knows how to find the center in himself and others, and he knows what strength and nourishment is there.

There is a lot of the philosopher in Jack. The first part of this clear and timely book reflects how deeply he has thought about his work and how far he has taken it. Jack goes beyond any of the models I'm familiar with. The truth that he speaks leaves me wondering how something so immediately recognized as true can go unrecognized so long. For a long time in structural bodywork, as well as in psychotherapy, we've had this explicit onion model of the body and a slightly less explicit one of the mind. We talk a lot of wholeness, but we've still got that compart-mentalizing habit: the mind in one box, the body in the other and both in layers.

Jack's book involves both mind and body, and he sees them as one. He sees this more truly than anyone before him. Let me quote: "Rather than viewing the body, the bodymind, as a many layered onion, I see it as a vibrant plastic mass, less viscous in some places than others, and coposed of the same interflowing stuff from outside to inside and inside to outside. Thus when touched at any level or depth, it instantaneously responds, reshaping itself in every other dimension and part."

Now that's wholism.

Nor does Jack think we can do one job at a time: change the body now, the mind later. It must be done

9

simultaneously, all at one on all levels. That's not the kind of thing you would hear from the departmentalist. And Jack has created a vehicle for this wholism in his work. He does work on body and mind together, in their "plastic mass." He does create changes that happen to the whole person. More than any other practitioner I know Jack puts into his practice and teaching all that his own mind and body can reach for and make happen.

It's one thing to do the work, to do it well, as an artist and healer. It's another to teach it and write about it. I remember another scene. Again, I think we were at Jack's house, though we could have been in Munich or Boulder. A bunch of people sitting around talking about the work, I suppose. One or two people spoke French and another German. The rest of us English. Most were Jack's students. He spoke to each in his or her language, switching easily from one language to another. That stuck in my mind, that scene. It seemed the epitomy of graciousness. That is, too, a part of the work and teaching. Meeting others on their own ground and terms.

Jack writes in this book about the contact between therapist and client. The therapist must have a presence and willingness to stay, to be honest and open, and to love. This is integral to the work. It's not technique, though skill is needed. It's even more than attitude. It's part of the very nature ofthe balanced and centered person that they come to important relationships as whole people, with everything they have and are. There's just no other way to do this work or to teach it.

Ron Kurtz
Hakomi School
Boulder, Co.

PROLOGUE

Search For Self Unity

Back in 1965, before I first became interested in working with the body, I was a professor of philosophy. I was very much in my head -- reading, speculating, and arguing with other intellectuals. My body and feelings were so neglected that, in revenge, they began sabotaging my intellectual life, making me unstable and confused. My muscles became tense and knotted and I developed chronic cramps and pains.   There I was, a young Ph.D., on my way to the top of my chosen profession, completely stuck-- my back swayed, hiding my sexual feelings; my legs turned out like a waddling, insecure baby; my shoulders hunched in constant fear; and my neck thrust forward with overeagerness.

At first I thought I could deal with my problems at a physical level. I sought relief from my tension by vigorous exercise -- swimming, tennis, basketball, and weight lifting. I became a great deal stronger, but also more tense and rigid. I then turned to hatha yoga, focusing on breath, stretching   exercises, and meditation. As I became proficient in doing yoga asanas, I did feel more relaxed and flexible, but my basic body attitude -- swayed back, turned out legs, hunched shoulders, and forward neck -- did not change very much. Nor did the physical, emotional, and intellectual parts of me seem more integrated. I controlled my emotional confusion more, but I was still divided, broken into parts that did not function together. Somehow, I said to my self, I have to go further.

I had heard of a revolutionary technique, called "Rolfing,"   after its creator, Ida Rolf, in which a practitioner, using very deep and painful manipulations, could straighten out crooked bodies. I was frightened at the prospect of submitting myself to anything which would hurt, but being desperate for relief from my misery, I signed up for a complete series of Rolfing sessions, which systematically dealt with different groups and layers of muscles. As my Rolfer used his knuckles and elbows to

11

reach those deep areas of my body that were crying out for relief, I experienced not only a release more satisfying and complete than ever before, I was also overwhelmed by old thoughts and feelings, long since forgotten, welling up into my consciousness. The fear that came over me at the death of my father, beatings at the hands of school bullies, the anger of being left by my mother -- all these memories came back with vivid force. I now felt my body as a locus, as a crucible for my emotions and ideas, but there were more feelings, more thoughts than I could hold and assimilate.

This was my introduction to what has become known as "bodywork," now a large field of disciplines, including much more than Rolfing, which works toward transforming the whole individual by direct work with the physical body. My posture went through many changes -- my legs and pelvis began to straighten -- but these physical changes were as insecure and temporary as my emotional and mental releases. I wanted deeper and deeper releases in every part of my body. I recognized that this work was evoking old, intense, and unresolved attitudes which I needed to deal with and integrate into more stable physical changes. For this reason I turned to emotional, but body oriented, therapy.

In "Reichian" therapy, named after an Austrian psychiatrist, Wilhelm Reich, I found an approach to self-transformation which helped me through much of my confusion. Whereas my Rolfer had been principally concerned with my physical alignment to gravity --letting the resulting emotions run their own course -- my Reichian therapist used bodywork to help me release and finish blocked feelings. Through a variety of breathing techniques -- panting, sighing, exaggerating diaphragmatic and upper chest inhalations, and forced exhalations -- I found my energy, my feelings and thoughts, building, and then climaxing into profound moments of relaxation, what the Reichians consider to be the natural rhythm of charging and discharging energy. All this was assisted by the timely interventions of my therapist. I was encouraged. I had begun to focus on one feeling at a time and was less confused.

Yet I missed the systematic physical restructuring, incomplete as it was, which I had been getting from Rolfing. Whereas my Rolfer had focused on the body, assuming that feelings would be properly affected, my Reichian therapist focused on feelings, assuming the body would find a good position and balance. During Reichian work, my body did get softer and more even in tone, but still lacked an easy upright balance. My experience with another emotional therapy, Gestalt therapy, developed by an Austrian psychiatrist, Fritz Perls, was similar. In Gestalt work I was encouraged to stay with, to feel, to express only what was happening now, right here -- to let my conflicting emotions enter into a dialogue, and find resolution by being more complete. Although my Gestalt therapist emphasized the importance of using the body, of expressing my feelings with it, the body was, for him, still an instrument for more emotional completeness, and I felt it was being partly neglected.

What started to dawn on me was that although I was now paying attention to my body and feelings, I was treating them as objects to be manipulated. My well-developed mental life was still subtly in control, seeing how far it could realize its plans by using the body and feelings to produce effects on each other. I was, in effect, separating my body and mind. I had first assumed that if my body could be tuned up like a machine, it would then give me pleasure and intellectual power. When this didn't fully work for me, I then said to myself: if I can just work through these confused emotions and thoughts, maybe my body will have a chance really to reshape itself.

I was beginning to see that it was this very attitude of doing something to the body, or to the mind, whether it be ignoing, strengthening, relaxing, or releasing them, that was the problem itself. And this is what part of this book is about: how we separate ourselves into body and mind, how we struggle vainly to reunite ourselves. I say vainly, because, as we shall see, we are already a single unity, one bodymind, which needs only to be recognized and accepted, not reunited.

The splitting of myself into body and mind had been a defense a kind of "armor," as the Reichians say, against the childhood memories and emotions I was now finally learning to confront. I had reinforced and secured this armor by creating a deep chronic contraction of the muscles around my neck and shoulders, cutting off my overactive head from my heart, from my need to be loved. I also had a contraction around my diaphragm, cutting off my heart from my unsatisfied sexual feelings. These were the hard, resistant defenses I had created for myself.

My armor also took a soft form. I had developed a kind of buffer against pain, a layer of protective fat around my belly and upper thighs. In these parts I was soft on the outside surface, but contracted and immobile on the inside, at the level of my deep muscles. I saw that I had created an imbalance between my outside and inner self, between my outer vulnerability and my inward, held-back anger. My Rolfer, and to a certain extent my Reichian therapist, had treated my body like an onion with layers which were to be peeled off from the outside toward the inside. But my feeling was that somehow my inside and outside self needed to be released together, not peeled, otherwise the armor released on the outside would simply shift toward the inside.

Recognizing my armor was a first step for me. But how was I to go further? I needed bodywork which none of the methods I had tried gave me. I needed a way to work with my bodymind as a unity, dealing with emotions, body, and thoughts all at the same time, not with one of them as a means to influence the others. I needed not only a way to deal with the hard, contracted defenses of my neck, shoulders, and diaphragm, but also a way to wake up the soft, unresponsive tissue of my thighs and belly, while at the same time, relaxing the underlying deeper tensions. Finally I saw that it was up to me to take responsibility for my own transformation.

There were two essential things that an intellectual life, a career as a professor of philosophy, didn't give me. I wanted to work with my hands, and I wanted direct physical and emotional contact with other people. It was the satisfying of these wants that would lead me on the path to discovery of my own unity. I saw that I could, though still incomplete myself, begin to work with and contact others, by becoming a bodyworker.

During this period of discovery I had no teachers. I simply followed my hands and intuition. I emersed myself in working with my friends, doing as many as 30 sessions a week. As I probed deep into connective tissue, the material enveloping and guiding the muscles, I encouraged my friends to play with their breathing -- fast and slow, hard and soft, deep and shallow -- to charge and discharge their energy. And as feelings surfaced I encouraged them to express directly what was happening at that moment. Gradually I was discovering how to time the rhythm of my work on deep tissue with the variations in breath and emotion. The changes amazed me. I hadn't realized that I could help bring about such rapid, complete, and lasting changes -- unitary, whole changes. And as I worked with my friends, I found myself breathing with them, sharing energy, feelings, and thoughts. I was working toward my own transformation and unity as well.

For me, "Postural Integration," the form of bodywork which I created from these experiences, and which I want to share with you in this book, is not an eclectic combination of techniques which I experienced or learned -- Rolfing, Reichian breathing, Gestalt, etc.; rather, it is a singular approach to the whole person. I found that when we change, we change throughout our whole being. We don't change physically, then mentally, or vice versa. We don't change a little on the outside, then later on the inside. When our changes are permanent and truly redirect our lives, we are transformed in all dimensions of the self at the same time. My experience starts from a whole, singular place where the experience of my body is the experience of my mind, where the experience of my inside self is the experience of my outside self. I can't divide and manipulate my experience; I can only flow with it, surrender to it. This was a frightening discovery for me, because I had to give up the idea of controlling myself and others.

As I came together in body and mind, inside and out, everything in my life was suddenly different. I felt a new freedom and flexibility which extended into my environment. The fear and insecurity of my childhood had kept me close to home and mother, and the university system was a safe refuge against an unpredictable world.

Now I was ready to break free from my academic life, to venture out of the South, where I grew up. I could travel, do bodywork anywhere I wanted to.

I felt like a pioneer. I started moving, working in different parts of the U.S. and finally, in countries all over the world. Compared to the more European culture of the East Coast and the South, which I had inherited, my new-found flexibility was really partly a frontier attitude. Many people, following the European mold, seem to treat their bodies as instruments which they keep healthy in pursuit of higher cultural values, values often requiring the restriction of staying with a few intellectual themes, in a limited number of physical locations.

As the frontiersman I had become, I was following the instincts and hunches of my whole self, letting my bodymind take me from one space to another -- the West Coast, Latin America, Quebec, Europe, Asia. In travelling, in feeling the space of other regions and foreign cultures, in seeing different character and body structures, I developed a broad and flexible view of the way in which I and my clients can change.

But there is, I discovered, another side to real transformation. It is not just that we change in every dimension of bodymind, both inside and outside of ourselves, we also, as we truly transform ourselves, find a center, a stable place or direction, in which our changes can happen with order and understanding. Deep bodywork helped me breakdown my old armor, the contractions dividing my head, heart, and desires. As my previous attitudes dissolved, I found myself accepting the natural flow of each new attitude into the next. When I allowed myself to be afraid, my fear exhausted itself, and changed into more aggressive feeling and action. It was only in trying to stop, and not completely experience any attitude, that I became confused about my direction. Stability and direction come, I gradually learned, in my accepting, even welcoming, newness and change.

At this time I was receiving weekly sessions of acupressure, a deep style of massage, applied along lines of energy, meridians, which connect all the parts of the bodymind in a complete circuit. After each session I felt every part of me subtly held together with a warm,

16

tingling vibration which sometimes lasted for days. At this time I also found that subtle movements of my body helped me to gain an unified image and feeling of my whole body. I took Alexander lessons, a method which helps one let go of predetermined goals about how to move, and I also got Feldenkrais sessions, a gentle method of encouraging the nervous system, through guided movements, to extend consciousness into even the smallest of actions. I found that I need not always be searching for grand transformations for me and my clients. Fine tuning and maintaining the flow of released energy was equally as important as the confrontation and breakdown of bodymind armor.

Finding and keeping a new, stable center was essential in my work with others. I could share myself and help others find a new direction, only if I was clear about my own direction. Even the harmony of society depends on the capacity of each of us to be   conscious of our own center. It is similar to sexual activity. When partners are too concerned about giving pleasure to each other, they are working against their own gratification. Our centers are not found in simple surrender to others, to family or society -- though acceptance and trust are important. For me, social harmony can eventually come only from individuals focusing on their own centers, on their own continuing needs.

In my work I found that when we as individuals begin to recognize and express our own needs, to find our centers, we want to confront, deeply touch, and share ourselves with others. (I consider the practice of Postural Integration, that is, working as a practitioner, simply an extension of this basic attitude, a method anyone willing to search for their own center can learn. I find it amusing, even ironic, and ultimately self-defeating that some groups of bodyworkers are so elitist that they refuse to believe that the average person has the sensitivity to learn to help others with deep touching.)

But if we are in an environment which makes it difficult to express and share our needs, we can either fight for bodymind freedom or change our environment. I have found that in our professions, homes, and in society in general that the people around us will, in fact, tolerate, accept and even eventually respect a great deal more openness, even confrontation and anger, than we in our armored thoughts would like to believe. It is convenient for us to say that we will lose our jobs and friends, if we really express and share ourselves. We overlook the movement and growth which happens in human relationships, especially when we express unpleasant attitudes.

There are, of course, circumstances where openness can result in loss of job, friends, and status, but that is part of healthy self-discovery. If we lose them because of our openness, we did not need them anyway. We can create a new environment that fits us. After having had around 20 sessions of deep bodywork, I could no longer tolerate the tension I was creating for myself as a university professor. Although I had tenure and was unsure what I could do outside the university for a living, I walked out and felt relieved. I was frightened but ready to accept my fear. I was soon amazed at how easily I created a new, centered and prosperous life for myself.

When we choose to remain in a certain environment, there is the continuing need for us to express our anxieties and frustrations. After the sweeping changes that one undergoes in deep bodywork, such as Postural Integration, one feels and is more quickly aware of tension, but having discovered how to charge and discharge any blocked energy, one can also get rid of it more easily. When centered, we may even sometimes choose to deal with an armored society in a deceptive way. In a totalitarian state, or the repressive parts in any society, we may choose not to be open about our needs. The question here is: how much can we manipulate elements of society and not manipulate ourselves? Each person, of course, has to discover these limits for him or herself.

****

I am now thumbing through **Common Ground**, Resources for Personal Transformation,* a catalogue of growth and healing practitioners and centers in the San Francisco Bay Area. More than five hundred centers and one hundred and fifty individuals are listed in categories including massage, naturopathic medicine, acupuncture,

18

herbal studies, biofeedback, colon hygiene, wholistic dentistry, vision improvement, deep tissue bodywork, neo-Reichian therapy, nutritional awareness, aikido, tai chi, psychic healing, Jungian dream work, past life therapy, and hypnosis. Obviously there is a renaissance of wholistic healing in the Bay Area. And I am delighted and amazed to find that whether my work takes me to London, Paris, Stockholm, Munich, Zurich, Geneva, Mexico City, Caracas, Cremona, Tokyo, Poona, Montreal, New Orleans, Chicago, New York, Seattle, or San Diego, scores of groups and individuals are also there, using these or similar approaches to healing. The renaissance is worldwide.

I have found many of these healing methods useful and have incorporated them into my own work. Anytime we come together with concern for each other, there is in some way movement toward human fulfillment. I am not disturbed that some over-enthusiastic practitioners claim inordinate healing power for themselves. We can learn, even from the over-optimistic. As I have learned in my own healing journey in company with thousands of clients, friends, and students, we can refine our sensitivity and techniques, and in so doing elevate our work to the level of art and science.

In this book I will share with you an attitude, an approach, a way of bringing together a variety of specific methods which is more than an eclectic combination, but is rather an effective, unified way to the direct, complete, and sustained unfolding of the whole person. In one sense I'm making a rather grandiose claim for this work. I believe, however, that it is one of the most effective paths available, and I invite you to join me in its exploration. My confidence derives from more than fifteen years of doing deep bodywork. In another sense I feel modest and am open to what others find effective. In fact, this is a fundamental condition of my approach. It is possible to help, to guide, to heal, only if we respect what is happening in each other, only if we allow each one of us to find his or her own singular response, expression and direction. Ultimately, all effective human transformation is nurtured by mutual respect and sharing.

This book is written for three levels of comprehension. First it is an introduction to "wholistic bodywork" for the beginner who does not understand how transformation of the body is also transformation of the whole person. There are a few technical charts, some anatomical terminology, and occasional references to special therapeutic methods, but these have been kept to a minimum.

Second, it is for the person who has already to some extent been exposed to the concepts of wholistic healing, but who wants to better understand its power and diversity or who may be interested in experiencing the process of Postural Integration. There are many case histories and other examples to help these readers get a clearer picture of the scope and variety of bodymind transformations. To help these readers, in each chapter I have given exercises which to help the reader begin to enter into the experience of bodywork.

Finally, there is material for the professionals -- the bodyworkers, therapists, counsellors -- who may be interested in how different methods can be applied simultaneously to the body, emotions, and thoughts. They will find a theoretical discussion of the nature of wholistic transformation, as well as specific illustrations of how individual changes can happen. Bodyworkers may be especially interested in the emphasis I have placed on Postural Integration as a step by step process and in my new classification, given in the last chapter, of bodymind types, based on my tactile experience.

I have faced two special semantic problems in the text. First, I have used the term "energy" to cover a range of activities. I take "energy" to be a primitive, undefinable term which can be understood when experienced. I have provided examples and exercises to help the reader sense its meaning. Second, in choosing a label for the person who undergoes Postural Integration, I did not want to use the medical term "patient," the experimental tag "subject," or the learning designation "model." Instead I have used the words "individual," "person," or "client." I initially rejected "client" but realized that a relationship with a client is as open and reciprocal as one wishes to make it, and after all, most of my work has been with clients. In the examples provided, I have given equal emphasis to both men and women. Not only has my clientele been more or less equally divided between men and women, the practitioners of Postural Integration include about thirty five to forty percent women, a rather high percentage considering that the work is thought of as requiring considerable size and strength.

I want to thank Michel Belair for encouraging me to undertake this book, Soma Jacobs and Don Donegan for their revisions.

*Common Ground, Resources for Personal Transformation, San Francisco: Summer 1986.

CHAPTER 1

TRANSFORMATION OF THE WHOLE SELF

This book is about how we can change ourselves. It is about a step-by-step process through which we can release the chronic tensions and frustrations which we have accumulated since infancy. It is about how we can open ourselves, letting blossom the vibrantly healthy and fully alive self which lies dormant in all of us. In this process toward more freedom and happiness we have to deal with our resistance to change. It may seem that most of us want to change, that we want to be more relaxed, healthier, more alive. But here lies the basic problem of human transformation. Although we say we want a different kind of life -- and may even be involved in many projects for improving ourselves -- there is a part of us which stubbornly resists any fundamental redirecting of our lives.

This part of us, which refuses to let go, is our armor. We call it armor because it is that aspect of us which, being afraid of possible pain and confusion, hardens or desensitizes our bodies and keeps our feelings and thoughts in careful control. Our armor is all those well-developed postures for dealing with life -- rigid neck, held in belly, fat, rubbery waist. It is all those guarded feelings -- covered up sadness, held-back anger, paralyzing fear. It is those often unstated but controlling beliefs -- If I try I'll be successful; if I'm kind to you, you should be kind to me.

Reflect upon your own behavior. Notice the little tricks for getting through the day; how you get yourself going in the mornings, how you keep high by not indulging in negative thoughts, how you put your best foot forward when you want to impress people. A large part of this behavior becomes second nature to us, set in motion unconsciously, and functions well for us up to a point as it protects us from pain and confusion. However, these habits also limit us and in the due course of time form a rigid structure, which then inhibits our spontaneity.

One of the main difficulties in changing ourselves is that this armor is largely unconscious but remains in control even as we try to modify a part of us. Each time we attempt to change our lives we are, in fact, using our already developed (and unconscious) postures and attitudes to deal with our problems. For example, if you over arch your lower back, creating severe backaches, you might try to find relief by doing yoga exercises. But you would probably concentrate on exercises which are easiest to execute and which at the moment feel good, such as arching your back even further into a fish or cobra position. In the long run such postures will simply increase your body imbalance and create more pain!

Here an unconscious attitude is driving you to find relief, but in a way which reinforces the old body position. Even if you are very disciplined and work with yoga positions which flatten your back, you will, through the attitude you carry throughout your body, simply transfer the tension and imbalance to another part of your body. In flattening out your back, you may round your shoulders and overcontract the muscles in your chest.

Or take another example. If you are very hard on the outside of your body, you may welcome very deep relaxing massage. You might, through frequent and thorough manipulation of this hard exterior begin to soften -- soften, that is, on the outside. Much of this outer tension would simply shift to deeper layers of muscle and tissue. You still have armor, only now you hold on to it deeper inside yourself.

You may have felt from time to time a similar type of self-control, a kind of incomplete relaxation. When you have gone for a long period of time under stress, you may have lost consciousness of how contracted your outer body has become. This hardness is a kind of defense against the discomfort of stress, but when the stress is past, and you become aware of the outer tension and are able to rest or even sleep, you may discover that you are left with a headache or inner nervousness which doesn't easily go away. Now that you're relaxed on the outside, you are even more conscious of a deeper, more persistent, inner discomfort.

These kinds of experiences show us that the tensions of the body are inseparable one from another, and are part of our overall posture and habits. Work on any part of ourselves which does not also release the whole structure, the habitual attitude behind our posture, is not transformation but simply a rearrangement of the problem. This is why, so often, we are simply exchanging the relief of one symptom for the creation of another. Our aching shoulders become lower back pains. Our back pains become bellyaches. All this becomes an endless chase of the cat after its own tail. And this is only at the level of physical discomfort.

When we go further and deal with the emotions and thoughts which are connected with our physical pains and imbalances, we encounter a similar subtle evasiveness. Whenever I say that I am willing to explore every part of my body and deal with my thoughts and feelings as well, I may be actually also using an unconscious part of my armor. Here there can be a hidden, implicit message: "I try, but nothing ever works for me" -- a message by which I manipulate my body and mind even when I believe I am releasing both.

In all our deliberate behavior there are such fundamental unconscious emotional and mental attitudes, which have developed along with our physical postures and which govern our well-intentioned efforts to improve our lives. Again we find relief for one emotion and its phsycial pain, only to find another emotional problem and physical symptom take their place. The headaches which accompany our outbursts of anger might disappear through sheer control of our anger, only to resurface as ulcers.

In the next chapter, "Inside And Outside Bodymind," I want to describe for you how and why we develop this kind of resistance to change, this kind of stubborn armor. But you may ask at this point: what kind of approach, what kind of process, can help against such deeply ingrained and often unconscious defenses? I have found in working with myself and with others that what we need is a way of dealing with the entire self, the unity of every part of our body, the outside together with the inside, the unity of our bodies with our minds and emotions.

As we change old, rigid body postures, we need also to change the accompanying rigid feelings and thought processes; or if we release blocked emotions and ideas, we need to free the muscles and tissues for new, more flexible movements. If for example, we want to change shoulders which chronically slump forward, we need to work not only with the tissue of the upper chest but also to work toward expressing our deeply entrenched attitude of being a burdened, helpless victim. And as we gain consciousness of the roles which we have been playing we also need to try out new emotions and physical positions of power and self-responsibility.

What I want to share with you in this book is a type of "bodywork"-- that is, a method which works directly with the muscles, the positions, the postures, and movements of the body -- but bodywork which is not just work on these physical aspects of the self but which also is direct work with the emotional and mental attitudes expressed by these physical activities. I call this method or process "Postural Integration."

In explaining Postural Integration to you I will be describing a specific process which I have developed, but I will also be describing any type of bodywork which respects what I see as three basic principles for unitary, whole, self-transformation. The first of these principles deals with the need to work with all aspects of the self at the same time, that is, simultaneously.

SIMULTANEOUS CHANGE

Orchestrating Bodymind

If you are unfamiliar with bodywork as a way of working toward transformation of the whole person, you might be surprised when visiting a session. There you might find a practitioner hovering over an individual, bearing down with hands, fingers, or elbows, while the person sighs, moans, or even screams and kicks. You might see the practitioner working very gently: rocking, cradling, and caressing the individual, encouraging deep

26

breathing, or perhaps entering into a dialogue of feelings and ideas. What sense could you make of all this? It might appear to be a cult, ritual, or even perversion.

When we recognize what stubborn creatures we really are, that we resist change at both the level of body and level of mind, we can begin to understand the need for such diverse and often surprising strategies. When we look at Postural Integration from one point of view we can see it simply as a bodywork in which the practitioner uses fingers, fists, and elbows to grip, twist, and shift layers of tissue and to reorganize the muscular system. But it is clearly much more.

We can't work with the body and assume that our thoughts and feelings will automatically flow more easily. We can't even begin to work with our bodies, if our minds are not cooperating. It is clear in the following example that the body is available, but only to the extent that the mind also permits.

Jim began by being evasive about almost everything. When directly confronted by anything unpleasant, he would find some way of avoiding or even running away from the problem. My first sessions with him were, in effect, pointless conversations, because he continually changed the subject. When I tried bodywork with him, he jerked away and cried, "Don't touch me," at even a very light touch. I explained that I couldn't help him in any way, if he was unwilling to confront himself and feel some pressure.

He made an agreement to allow me to increase my pressure slightly, while he continued to moan and groan, but not move away. After several sessions of this light work, which included a great deal of slow meditative breathing, he finally allowed me to increase the pressure, and I was able to complete what I considered to be the first session of deep work. Thereafter he was more receptive to deep work in each session, and began sharing feelings of loneliness which he had held beneath his initial, protective reactions.

At this point it is important to undertand that wholistic bodywork is not just a matter of making sure that we work with both mind and body, as nearly everybody claims they are doing, but has to do with the fact that body and mind are uniquely joined, that they are in fact inseparable, and have to be dealt with at the same time. The self is a rich symphony of sensations, feelings, ideas. And as one aspect of us comes to the fore, we may call it the "body," as another draws attention, it becomes "mind." But both are dependent on the full orchestrated background of the self.

You can see this from my previous discussion. In the Prologue I recounted how my attempts to deal with my mental confusion by releasing my body and my attempts to balance my body by working through my feelings and thoughts -- all were unsuccessful attempts to find a complete and satisfying change in my life. I was trying to use one part of my self, with all its previously developed habits and attitudes, to change another part of my self. I was trying to use either body or mind to manipulate myself. When we recognize we are a single unity, one "bodymind," we begin to understand that we cannot finally manipulate one part of ourselves with another. When we work with the body we are also at the same time working with the mind, or when working with the mind we are in fact in some way touching the body -- they are simply different aspect of the same unity, different ways of focusing on the same experience.

Here is an exercise you can use to explore how your body and mind are parts of the same experience.

> **Have a friend use both arms around your waist to lift you off and put you back on the floor. Notice how heavy you are. Without telling your partner what you are doing, relax and take several deep breaths. Imagine that you are very, very heavy -- perhaps that you are a pile of heavy metal, or an elephant. Become this image in your feelings and thoughts. Take the image into your torso, legs, and arms. Have your friend lift you again. Notice how much more difficult it is for him to lift you. Try also being light.**

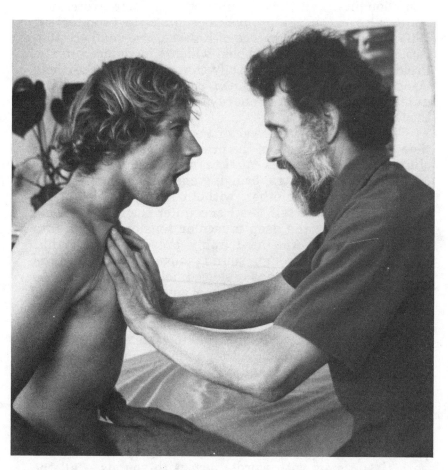

In wholistic bodywork the practitioner recognizes that in touching the body there is also contact with feelings and thoughts, and that one must encourage the espression of these in bringing about a physical change. The practitioner and client work together, now with tissue, now with sounds or words -- all the time recognizing the physical, emotional, and cognitive unity of the process.

Postural Integration, as a form of wholistic bodywork, is **bodymind** or **mindbody** work. The practitioner recognizes that in touching the body, either superficially or deeply, there is also contact, **simultaneously**, with both feelings and thoughts, and that in encouraging their expression one is also encouraging physical change. In Chapter III, "The Process and Experience of Release," we shall see that Gestalt and Reichian methods, which I introduced in the Prologue, are important to body change because they help bring out of the body the hidden, controlling attitudes, and unleash the held-back energy of unclaimed, armored thoughts and feelings.

The extraordinary power of Postural Integration lies, then, in the willingness of the practitioner to work with the client on many levels at the same time. It is like conducting an orchestra, bringing one section of the self to the fore, and then another, without losing a sense of the full harmony of the self. As I encounter the body with my hands, loosening the deep muscular tensions, I look into my client's eyes. And as I apply pressure, I ask that person to share through sound, movement, and words what is happening -- what is sensed, felt, and thought. As Richard Heckler of the Lomi School says in **The Anatomy of Change**, "Working through the body we contact the person and their energy in the way they gesture and move, the sound of their voice, their urge toward or away from contact, their posture, how they respond under pressure, and how their images and thoughts are translated into action." (1)

By maintaining this contact, this open sharing, the practitioner can be flexible enough to change the emphasis of the work to meet the changing demands of the whole person. The practitioner and client together, now work with tissue, now with words, now with sounds -- all the time recognizing the physical, emotional, and cognitive unity of the process. My experience has been that when either the practitioner or client is holding back part of him or herself -- even as a part of the self to be dealt with at a later time -- the changes which do occur are partial, temporary, or even disorganizing.

I emphasize that healing transformation is simultaneous change, because I have noted that there is a

30

tendency among some healers to treat body and mind as if they are objects which affect each other causally over a period of time. There is a temptation to assume that if we work to restructure the body in a new physical form, we will eventually bring about healthier feelings and thoughts. And conversely if we can get emotionally and mentally balanced, the effect, it is thought, will be to release our physical stress.

There are some bodyworkers, for example, who seek to bring the sections of the body into balance in relation to the earth's gravitational field. Legs, pelvis, torso, and head are seen as the sections or blocks, which because of stress shift out of efficient alignment. They assume that if the sections of the body find a careful and precise balance, that the emotions will also be harmoniously affected. The work of these same practitioners is often subtle and masterly in its use of careful hand maneuvers, yet in my experience this approach leaves aspects of the self out of realignment. For me, physical manipulations which are not simultaneously part of emotional and cognitive change result in superficial and temporary rearrangements of some of the parts, instead of a complete and instantaneous restructuring of the whole self.

It is true that when the whole self, the entire bodymind, is free and centered, we are also in physical harmony with gravity, but we can never achieve this physical balance, unless our changes begin happening in every dimension of us at the same time. There is no way we can first find physical balance and subsequently catch up emotionally and mentally.

Jane was a one hundred mile long distance runner. She felt no strain or exhaustion as she ran. She could run until she suddenly collapsed. She once did not realize she had broken a bone in her foot until after the race. During the first session of bodywork she felt no pain, nor expressed any emotion, no matter how hard the pressure. Her tissue was rubbery and although not hard, it was evasive and resistant to movement. There seemed to be no conscious connection between what she felt in her body and what was going on in her emotions

31

and thoughts. The few "changes" she did feel she recognized days later, but these effects were quickly lost. She was out of synch with herself. I felt something more could happen but decided to simply work carefully on the layers of tissue.

After several sessions, I felt the need to be more provocative, to show her my impatience. As I scratched the surface of her body, she became red-faced and began to cry out, angry and demanding, like a newborn baby. Her consciousness immediately was in stride with her fast running body. Her body became supple and receptive. She spoke of her sadness. As we shared a new found energy, the previously separated parts of her continued to come together.

This principle of simultaneity which is vital for working with body and mind as a single unit is also valid in working with both the inner and outer parts of our selves. In Chapter II I will explain how we develop an outside shell and inner core to protect us against possible painful experience. The creation of a core and shell is another way that we manipulate ourselves. We tend to separate and isolate our inner and outer experiences, rather than opening to their simultaneous power. We often believe that if we can handle one part adequately, the other half will follow suit.

This happens physically and mentally. At the physical level we may develop the outer muscles of the body, what are anatomically called the extrinsic muscles. These are the large powerful muscles of locomotion, which power the movements in running, lifting, and throwing. We may develop these outside muscles as a method of overcoming our problems through sheer power and strength, but in the process we overpower our inner muscles, the intrinsics, which initiate and coordinate our outer movements. This imbalance, between a hard shell and soft core, in the extreme, would leave us muscle bound, outwardly stiff and clumsy. And at the emotional level, we might believe that if our lives are active enough on the outside, they will be active enough on the inside.

The jaws hold tension which is not merely the accumulation of physical stress. They hold anger and anxiety which we cannot fully release at the physical level alone. Also the stress we feel on the outside of the body around the jaws is part of what is happening deep inside ourselves at a visceral level.

Place the fingertips of both hands on your upper jaws just under the cheek bones. Press firmly and slowly with equal pressure on both sides, letting your fingers go through the surface tissue of the cheeks until you feel the resistance of the masseter muscle (which runs from the cheek down to the lower jaw). You may feel this resistance as a hardness or soreness. Increase your pressure until you begin to feel discomfort.

Notice that at this point you may find any number of defensive reasons for not continuing your pressure. You might find yourself saying that the force is too great to bear, that you may be harming yourself, or that feeling pain is not worth any dubious benefits. Such a defensive, armored attitude is a part of the physical tension and would be preventing you from softening and releasing all the held-back emotions locked in the jaws.

Now release your pressure and prepare to try again with a different attitude. First build your energy by breathing deeply for several minutes. While opening and closing your jaws explore various sounds of fear and anger. Press again on the upper jaws. As you begin to feel discomfort, let your sounds become louder cries or shouts. As you feel more discomfort or pain, let these sounds come from deep in your belly and stay with any emotions welling up inside you. Notice that you can now apply more pressure with less avoidance, that when you are completely expressing yourself, what was uncomfortable or painful, becomes a welcome release. Body and mind, as well as inside and outside, are all being transformed at the same time.

If we become conscious of the overdevelopment of the outside of ourselves, of the hard protective shell we have created, we might try to soften this defense by working gradually from the outside toward the core. One of the most frequently used strategies in deep bodywork is to work from the shell to the core. In this work the body is considered to be layered like an onion, and in order to affect and reach the inside layers, the outside has to be peeled away.

We can understand this approach to the body better, if we look, for a moment, at the nature and arrangement of the tissue being manipulated. As I shall explain in more detail in the next chapter, the muscles of the body are wrapped in envelopes, consisting of a pliable tissue called fascia. This material organizes and guides our muscles by forming a system made of layers of tissue. On the outside of the body we have a large, all-encompassing layer, which like a big shopping bag, holds everything together.

As we go deeper we find individual sheaths for each muscle. As we develop rigid physical and emotional patterns of behavior, this system of fascia becomes less flexible, restricting our movements and overall bodymind attitude. The strategy in this kind of work from outside toward inside is to soften and reorganize those parts of the fascial system which have become hard and stuck, and this, in turn, it is thought, gives mobility and balance to the muscles held in the fascia.

However, I have found that if we begin working with the outside of ourselves in the belief that we can affect and make more available our insides, we overlook how our armor subtly shifts its defenses. The tension that we release superficially may simply move toward a deeper more protected place. It is, of course, important to respect the rate at which a person undergoes and assimilates change, and often in my work I focus on the outside superficial planes of fascia, and then gradually go deeper. Yet I have found that when real transformation occurs, it is not only the outside that is changed. The inside is also simultaneously undergoing corresponding changes.

As I begin working with superficial layers of tissue, I am coordinating this work with the individual movement of intrinsic muscles, such as gentle rocking of the pelvis or short, slight movements of the spine. Also as I work with

34

the extrinsic musculature, as well as the outer feelings and attitudes, I may, for example, work simultaneously inside the mouth, which holds some of the deepest structures, emotions, and attitudes of the body. Rather than viewing the body, the bodymind, as a many layered onion, I see it as a vibrant, plastic mass, less viscous in some places than others, and composed of the same interflowing stuff from outside to inside and from inside to outside. Thus when touched at any level or depth, it instantaneously responds, reshaping itself in every other dimension and part.

Greta had grown up in the slums of London. She had a tough outer and inner attitude toward the world. During the beginning of each session she was stoic, in effect saying, "I can take anything you can dish out." As I worked she gritted her teeth and refused to admit she felt any pain at all. I encouraged her to stay with and even exaggerate this feeling of being tough, while I worked at the same time working inside her mouth provoking a gagging reflex which moved in rippling spasms from her belly to her throat. After this or similar work in each session, her outer body would become softer to the touch and she reported a release deep in her guts and throat. Gradually she became responsive and expressive at the beginning of the sessions as well.

In Chapter IV, "The Process and Experience of Release," I outline how we can change gradually but simultaneously throughout all the dimensions of ourselves, how we can change in body and mind, as well as inside and out. We shall see that we can improve from one moment to the next, but our transformation is from the unity experienced a moment ago to the unity we continue to enlarge and enhance in the present moment.

The changes do not occur first in our bodies and later in our feelings and thoughts, or first on the outside then later on the inside. We change simultaneously in bodymind, inside and outside, or fall into the deception of viewing ourselves as fragmented parts. We shall see that the

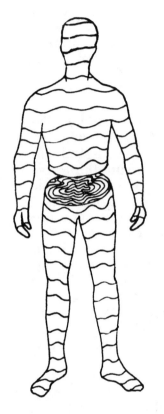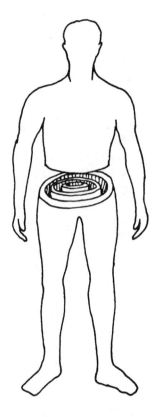

The body can be viewed as similar to an onion with layers of tissue. But this view tends to reinforce the idea that we are made up of parts which need to be released separately and individually. Actually, the body is more like a vibrant, plastic mass, less viscous in some places than others, but made up of the same interflowing stuff. When touched at any level or depth, it instantaneously responds, reshaping itself in every other dimension and part.

practitioner can follow a strategy of focusing on one part or depth of the body at a time, without losing contact with the emotional and mental dimensions of the self and without violating its inner and outer unity.

To sum up, the first principle of my wholistic approach to bodywork is: all lasting human growth is simultaneous change in every aspect of ourselves, in both body and mind, in both the inner and outer parts of ourselves.

BALANCED CHANGE

Encouraging A Continuous Flow In The Self

I have explained that Postural Integration, as a wholistic form of bodywork, is a way of releasing our rigid postures, those half forgotten physical, emotional, and mental habits we have developed for coping with the stresses of living. On the other hand, it is also an integration, because it is a process which assists us in the assimilation of new found energy and freedom into our lives. When we become more conscious and begin to sit, stand, walk, feel and think more spontaneously, we don't necessarily completely give up our old postures and patterns. We can still slouch, come to attention, be pessimistic or optimistic, but there is now no need to become stuck in any of these patterns. They are no longer the narrow focus from which we force ourselves to see and experience life.

We can now try out new movements, explore new feelings and attitudes, until they too, become habitual, and can be replaced (but not given up) by spontaneous behavior. We can liken this activity to the charging and discharging of a battery. As we discipline ourselves into habits, we store energy; as we surrender to new experience, we release this stored energy. This building of energy, its discharge, and recharge is a continuously repeated cycle. If we refuse to charge ourselves, we remain weak, looking for more energy. If we refuse to discharge, we become tense with the excessive, held-back energy. Allowing the

37

cycle of charge and discharge to flow in all the activities of our bodymind gives us a natural, ever-present direction.

This cycle of charge and discharge involves both the old and the new. I accept and use my past habits and attitudes, but I am free to be spontaneous. Each movement, each emotion, each idea takes the necessary space and energy to complete itself, but does not block the activity of the next moment. For example, as I begin to feel my anger, I need time for the irritation to grow, time for my energy to charge. And as my anger mounts I need time to fully express it, to allow it to discharge. If my building irritation or the peak of my anger is cut short, I am left stuck in my frustration. Or if I continue to express my anger until it becomes a senseless rage, I become stuck in my exhaustion.

You might try the following exercise:

Place a mattress on the floor in a room where you will not be disturbed and where you have the freedom to make any movements and sounds you want. Lie on your back and follow the rhythm of your breathing. Allow yourself to gradually increase the rate of your breathing, beginning slowly and going faster. Focus on inhaling as much air as you comfortably can, then as you reach your fastest rhythm, begin exhaling forcefully with a quick sound.

Stay with whatever feeling might come up. If you are angry, express your anger by shouting or moving. If you feel sad, let yourself cry or curl up. After you have fully expressed whatever feelings may have arisen, notice if you feel complete. If not, try the whole process again, until you feel you have finished the feeling.

After feeling complete, notice whether it is now easier to allow new feelings to follow the feelings which you completed -- whether softness, or fragility may follow anger, whether power or determination may follow sadness, etc.

As we release our blocked habits we allow for more charge or discharge, but the sudden new movement of our energy can be disorienting unless we learn to allow our energy to run its course and find a new balance or harmony. As I explain in Chapter III, the first stage of Postural Integration is the release of our rigid structures; the second stage is the integration, the harmonizing of the new energy. After releasing their blocks, I want my clients to focus on the connections in their lives, to feel how they can flow from one movement, feeling or thought to another without having to hold on to old postures and attitudes. I work with the overall form of bodymind, organizing the long fascial planes and sheaths between major body segments. The legs and thighs can now undulate together with the breathing movements of the torso. The pelvis can naturally rock with the head.

In this integrating stage, as we shall see in Chapter IV, "Breath, Balance, and Energy," when breathing is free, there is a balance between inhalation and exhalation, between our capacity to charge and discharge our energy. While working with the fascia, I respect the individual's breathing rhythm, letting my pressure follow and adjust to the range of inhalation and exhalation. What I describe as "spontaneous breathing," that is, a vibrating, unpredictable movement of the whole breathing apparatus and eventually the entire body, is essential to the individual's continuing balance and flexibility.

Frank had lived most of his life in a small rural southern town. He had had a strict religious and moral upbringing, and his body was as stiff and rigid as his character. Now he was in San Francisco, and as I took him through the first seven sessions of Postural Integration, which emphasize the release of armor, he let go of much of his body tension and repressed emotion. He discovered it was o.k. for him to breathe rapidly, become excited, and discharge his energy.

After the seventh session, which completed the releasing emphasis of the work, he felt freer and more flexible, but somewhat confused and off-balance. Although no longer over controlling himself with his old attitudes, he had not yet found a new direction. One feeling after another poured

out of him. He was discharging in many directions but not recharging.

In the final three sessions I worked to connect his grounding with his upper half, by alternately working with his ankles and knees, on the one hand, and with his arms and neck, on the other. I asked him to focus on slow breathing and on staying with one feeling until it had time to more completely run its course, without denying any of the feelings that might follow. Gradually he began to give himself more time and his body movements started to reveal a new harmony. His breath was now soft, deep, and vibrant.

Although integration is emphasized in the second stage of this bodywork process, the releases during the first stage also needs to be accompanied by a certain degree of integrative work. In the prologue I mentioned how, along with the freeing of my basic bodymind blocks, it was important for me, using acupressure and movement awareness to finely adjust the energy which I had already released. In other words, along with the coarse overall changes in my body form and character structure, I needed to begin a fine tuning, an integration of the massive changes I was undergoing. In Chapter V, "Integrating And Fine Tuning Bodymind," I discuss how to use such diverse methods as acupressure, Gestalt, and movement awareness to integrate different aspects of bodymind: right-left, front-back, and top-bottom.

To summerize this introduction to balanced change, I offer a second principle to guide wholistic bodywork: in order for us to maintain and improve upon the unified, simultaneous changes we undergo, we need to develop balance and direction, a center from which we not only accept old patterns but develop new possibilities and through which we allow our energy to move continuously in cycles of charge, discharge, and recharge.

CHANGE AS AN INTERACTION BETWEEN PRACTITIONER AND CLIENT
The Give And Take Of Sharing

There is another kind of unity which needs to be respected, if the transformation of the self is to be effective and whole. Consider the contact in deep bodywork between the practitioner and client.

I find it is often the case that either a client or a practitioner does not really want to enter into a clear and complete exchange. Often they have the idea that they can receive or give the help needed without letting go of a carefully guarded part of themselves. Maybe sometime you have gone to someone with the idea that you're going to be helped without having to reveal or confront what's going on inside. Maybe you have encountered so-called therapists or healers who remain aloof, who were not about to reveal any personal part of themselves as they work with you. In deep bodywork this lack of sharing and interaction prevents any genuine change.

This failure to share takes different forms. Sometimes the practitioner or client may want to interact at only a physical level, but then the ignored emotions will subvert the sought physical changes. Or if the contact is an outer contact, without any inner movement, the inside will resist any changes that are being attempted on the outside. If my fear is so great that I have withdrawn my sensitivity and responsiveness, very little can happen, even if the practitioner does everything conceivable. Or if I need sympathy from the practitioner and he or she is just doing the job on the outside of me, the unfulfilled part of me will not allow the tissues to open and change.

Let us consider for a moment the practitioner working with an individual's breathing. In working toward free, spontaneous breathing, the practitioner needs to work at the person's own pace or rhythm. It is not enough to mechanically apply pressure to the rib cage or diaphragm. If the client is to surrender a well-developed armor and find a new but centered direction, he or she has to be given the time and space to accept the contact, pressure, and movements initiated by the practitioner. And for the practitioner to sense the degree of acceptance, the pace at which significant and lasting change can take place, he or she needs to be balanced in bodymind, allowing the energy to flow to and from the client. But also if there is to be any movement beyond an armored attitude, the client needs to be willing to follow some of the new directions offered by the practitioner.

This kind of exchange or sharing needs to happen, not just while working with breathing, but within each moment of contact -- when tissue is being released, when the expression of emotions is being encouraged, when thoughts are being explored.

> **Maria is a housewife in Caracas. Coming from a wealthy upperclass family, she expected things to be done for her. She came to the sessions with the attitude that I should tell her what was wrong and then fix the problem. She lay impassively on the table as I began to work. I suggested that she consider whether she was playing a role of being passive, helpless, or even burdened. I saw that she needed to be on her feet, moving with me, so I braced myself against the wall and invited her to press her body into my hands and to express openly any kind of sound or feeling coming up inside her. She soon found that she, herself, could move at the appropriate angle and force to reach and release the tensions in her body. The work became a beautiful dance between us, with her often suggesting where my hands would be most effective and she began sharing feelings of how she was often frustrated and stuck.**

This kind of interaction or sharing, which is vital for whole transformation, can also be thwarted by an attitude that there is an "objective" approach to changing the individual. It is sometimes thought that if one analyzes the structure of an individual, one can determine the nature of the problems, use the appropriate methods, and afterwards evaluate the degree of success. Even if the client wants this kind of treatment, he or she is being manipulated and there is no real interaction with the practitioner and consequently no lasting transformation.

The temptation to treat the client as an object is especially great when "reading" the structure of the body or character. Many writers have classified individuals into certain types: into body types, such as those offered by Ron Kurtz (2), or into psychiatric or character types, such as those offered by Freud, Jung, Reich, or Lowen.(3) The body is seen as perhaps top-heavy or bottom-heavy, that is, with one half overly developed. Or the personality is, perhaps, viewed as being masochistic, or narcissistic.

As we shall see in Chapter VI, "Between You and Me, Sharing and Transforming Energy," it is possible to use these classifications if the practitioner and client treat them as possible, but not fixed, ways of understanding and guiding the interaction which is happening between them. Rather than type-casting a client, which is a joint confirmation of the armor of both client and practitioner, it is important to stay open to all the possibilities for change.

Claudio is a Milanese businessman, an "eager beaver," and very successful in high pressure sales work. When I began to work with him he moved too much, too rapidly, and too enthusiastically for me to grip and soften the tissue. He thought that if I could just give him an exact diagnosis of what was wrong and what he should do that he could take care of any of his difficulties.

I pointed out two possibilities. He could let himself continue at this rapid pace, deliberately increase the feelings and movements, even to the point of hysteria, or he might slow down everything. He decided to try to slow down. I then began each session with meditative breathing and movement. I stopped working immediately each time he became rushed, until we at last discovered a level of exchange where he was able to feel more than superficial, protective, and rushed activity. I was able to sense his acceptance of my need to work more slowly.

In order to get in touch with the importance of sharing in changing yourself, try the following:

Arrange with a good friend to receive a massage. Set up the environment just the way you want it -- heating, lighting, music, all appropriate. During the massage make a point to ask for what you want. Whether you want to be massaged deeper or softer, slower or faster. Ask your partner how he or she feels giving the massage and what kind of strokes are nicest to give. Be sure to discuss any negative feelings which either of you may feel -- even if these seem trivial. Notice at the end of the massage how you feel -- whether you feel more satisfaction or relaxation than at the end of other massages you have had.

The final principle for unitary change is: if the individual is to undergo unified and centered transformation, the practitioner and individual need to allow a free and complete interaction with each other.

I do not wish to claim that I have been able perfectly to follow these three principles of transformation in every moment of my work. But I feel that they explain the direction in which I am working and that when, indeed, my work does help someone to improve the quality of their life, I have been in some way approaching the ideal of these principles.

FOOTNOTES FOR CHAPTER I

1. **The Anatomy of Change**, Richard Strozze Heckler, (Boulder: Shambhala, 1984) p. 17.
2. **The Body Reveals**, Ron Kurtz and Hector Prestera, M.D. (New York: Harper and Row, 1976).
3. See the following:**Character Analysis**, Wilhelm Reich (London: Vision Press, 1950).
   The Physical Dynamics of Character Structure, Alexander Lowen (New York: 1958).

Also for a review of some of the types of Freud and Jung see:
Know Your Type, Ralph Metzner (New York, 1979).

CHAPTER II

INSIDE AND OUTSIDE BODYMIND

When deep bodywork respects the need of the individual for wholeness and unity, it is a powerful way for restoring our health, flexibility, and spontaneity. But first, we may ask, what keeps us from naturally experiencing the unity of our bodies and minds? Why do we separate ourselves into outer and inner selves? Why do we refuse to share fully our energy with others?

I want to begin answering these questions by looking at how we inhibit or even stop our natural tendency to change with the demands of our environment and looking at how, as far back as foetal development, infancy and childhood we begin to armor ourselves against certain kinds of growth and spontaneous change. Once it is clear how we split ourselves into armored parts, I will then present a view in which bodymind is seen as a single, indivisible reality, a unity in which our inside and outside selves function harmoniously together, and can be shared with others. In the next chapter I will begin to introduce you to some of the techniques by which we can release our blocks and unify ourselves.

GROWTH AND PROTECTIVE ARMOR
Refusing To Grow Up

Let us look for a moment at human growth. We continuously change as we pass from conception, through gestation, infancy, childhood, maturity, middle age, old age, and finally death. These changes at each stage of life can be in harmony with our lives and our environment or they can be changes with which we create frustration, incompleteness, and rigidity. What we need in youth for harmonious change may be completely inadequate for us as adults. Our physical forms in childhood simply are inadequate to handle the needs of solid muscular adults.

Our growing bodies, as well as society, constantly place new demands on us. The demands are often so great that many of us simply refuse to "grow up." And our bodies reveal where and when we stopped ourselves.

Take for example, the man with large, powerful arms and chest who has the thin legs of a young boy, or the woman with broad hips and full thighs whose breasts are still preadolescent. Conversely, we can get ahead of ourselves causing parts of us to age too rapidly, as can be seen in young people who already have the wrinkles of middle age across their brows.

Our refusal to flow with harmonious change initially begins as a way for us to protect ourselves against harm and pain. When sensing that we are about to be attacked, we may tighten physically, emotionally, and mentally to meet the threat, or if our fear is overwhelming, we may paralyze ourselves to avoid provoking harm. These responses to danger, or pain, are natural ways of protecting ourselves against our environment.

It is only when we begin to anticipate events and develop a habitual response to a danger not present that we create an overprotective attitude. If you are in a state of perpetual preparedness, your tissue and muscles will become chronically overcontracted. If you are afraid to react because of the hurt which may follow, you will become unresponsive and flaccid. We can see that when our natural protective system (although no longer appropriate) becomes a habitual part of our bodies and attitudes, we have developed an armor against living in the present moment.

In the process of growing up, we may protect ourselves against hurt by tightening or paralyzing ourselves, not only physically, but emotionally and mentally as well. Rather than confront the possibility of further pain in dealing with our parents or society, we repeatedly use the same mechanism until the reason for its use has become unconscious to us. And we continue to use this same armor after there is not even a remote threat. We constantly relive the past because it seems familiar and safe, rather than opening ourselves to the present problems, satisfactions, and joys of life. It is this stubborn

48

refusal to let go of the past which creates our misery and leads to illness and premature death.

Moshe Feldenkrais has observed that

> **The habit formation mechanisms are operative in all of us; why are we not then all neurotic? The answer is that most of us are .... Most of us stick to some infantile pattern which is so charged with emotional tension that we cannot even consider the possibility of it being wrong. Our attitudes toward the body functions, work, society, pleasure are rarely rational. They are, most of the time, perpetuations of an old emotionally established pattern and indicate arrested development in one direction or another.(1)**

Wilhelm Reich, originally a member of Freud's circle of disciples, saw armor as forming in rigid bands around our body. Our natural spontaneous movement, a fine vibration or streaming of energy and feeling throughout the body, is broken by these immobile segments around the eyes, mouth, throat, chest, diaphragm, belly, and pelvis. Each band of armor holds a part of our character, our habitual way of coping with ourselves and society. Reich saw armor as a rigidity of emotional response, accompanied by contractions of the musculature.(2) But armor can also be unresponsiveness and consist of tissue which is loose and flaccid. In both the case of hard or soft armor, we suppress, to a large extent, our consciousness of the attitudes which we have locked in body and mind.

Try the following as a way better to see and understand your own armor:

> **Take photographs of yourself (front, side, and rear views). With a marker draw bands across each of the segments in the photograph -- eyes, mouth, throat, chest, diaphragm, belly, and pelvis. List all the emotions you see held in these bands. Now one band at a time, express the feeling indicated while looking in the mirror. Which bands do you find the most immobile? Do they seem to reinforce the armor**

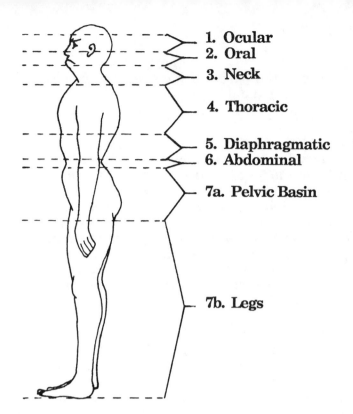

1. Ocular
2. Oral
3. Neck
4. Thoracic
5. Diaphragmatic
6. Abdominal
7a. Pelvic Basin
7b. Legs

As a natural response to pain or danger we may tighten or paralyze ourselves. Armor (overly contracted or excessively soft tissue) develops from our habitual responses, which form when we begin to anticipate a danger which is no longer really present. Armor can be looked at as physical, emotional, and mental segments which encircle the body and block its flexible and spontaneous movement. Here we see seven segments or bands of armor: 1) the ocular segment forms a defense which includes contraction, stiffness, or immobility around the scalp, forehead, eyelids, eyeballs, and tear glands and reveals a frozen, masklike or empty expression; 2) the oral segment includes the lips, chin, and throat and holds repressed needs to suck, bite, and yell; 3) the neck segment often holds back anger and swallowed feelings; 4) the thoracic segment can be stiff with controlled, pulled back shoulders or collapsed with chronic sorrow and weakness; 5) the diaphragmatic segment may cut the upper half of the person from the lower, not allowing the head and heart above, to connect with the pelvis, below; 6) the abdominal segment is around the intestines, stomach, pancreas, liver, and kidneys and holds deep gut feelings such as disgust and fear of dying; 7) the pelvic segment has two parts, 7a, the pelvic basin, which holds our deepest sexual longings and frustrations, and 7b, the legs, which hold our insecurities and lack of grounding.

50

in neighboring bands? Does a band separate major parts of your body from another? How do you feel in the two parts?

Our body shape, physical movement, emotional expression, and thought all reveal the history of our growth, a history which is our degree of success in being continually responsive to new needs, as well as our degree of failure in letting go of the past. We develop rigid or unresponsive postures or attitudes, and even though we may attempt to conceal them from the world or from ourselves, the rigidity always is apparent to the sensitive observer.

There is no way we can hide that angry and frightened little boy or girl inside of us, just as there is no way we can hide the power and ability which we have already developed. The incomplete parts of us are always present, but we try our best to make them unconscious and separate. When I look in the mirror, it is easy for me to hold my belly nice and flat, but I avoid seeing and feeling how I cut off my diaphragmatic breathing. It is easy for me to look down at my big, broad feet, and instead of accepting their support and balance, be resentful that they are not graceful and beautiful.

Our armor is largely unconscious, because we try to cope with our pain and dissatisfaction by looking at ourselves as a set of habitual responses, as a mechanism which we can manipulate. When I say of a pain in my shoulder, "It hurts me," I treat my body as an object which is doing something to me. I may succeed in suppressing this pain by diverting my attention or taking a pain reliever. However, as long as I deal with a part of myself as an object, I am only temporarily rearranging my behavior, instead of confronting and opening to the pain as an important dimension of my overall experience. We clearly, also turn our emotions and thoughts into objects, as when we encourage someone who is holding back to "let go of it," or when we tell a confused person to "think it through."

51

The manipulation of ourselves as objects takes two principal forms: the splitting of the self into body and mind, and the separating of the inner from the outer part of the self. Let us examine the first.

BODYMIND AND MINDBODY
True Monism

Our unwillingness to give up the security of the past leads us to deal with ourselves as divided, as "body" and "mind," as two parts which somehow affect each other. We may consider our bodies as a means to emotional stability or mental clarity. We may discipline it and care for it, but as long as we view it as something to be manipulated we are avoiding, resisting, the problems that lie beneath our armor.

Hans lived in Munich. He had been an exercise nut his whole life. He played soccer, hockey, skied, and lifted weights. He was careful with his diet and took vitamins. His general attitude was that if he stayed strong and healthy, everything would work in his life. His body was powerful but stiff and in some places nearly muscle bound. In recent years he felt a great deal of pain in his ankles. As I worked with the hard, well-developed muscular structure (the armor) around his ankles, he began to cry, then relaxed. He expressed how he had spent most of his life standing his ground against his father, and covering up the deep hurt he had felt at not being accepted and loved. He had been treating himself as a physical object, denying the loneliness and emptiness beneath his athletic rigidity.

We may also attempt to use emotional or mental clarity as a way of controlling our physical lives. We assume that if we can adequately develop the powers of the mind, we can control the function of our body.

Nicole is from a famous Parisian family. She is highly disciplined in her mental and spiritual life. She turned every negative thought into a positive affirmation. But during the previous year she had complained of internal cramps and constipation. As I worked with her, loosening the large adductor muscles of the inner thigh, she began to shake and jerk in confusion and excitement. She was surprised to discover, contrary to her polite upbring, that it was alright for her to be confused and excited. She has been using her mind as an instrument to control herself, but her body rebelled, venting normal but accumulated tensions.

You may have noticed in the previous discussion and examples, I have sometimes classified the emotions with the body, sometimes with the mind. This difficulty demonstrates how we cannot classify the self into independent parts, even when we claim that these parts are interrelated. I view the self as a functional, inseparable whole which incorporates the physical, emotional, and mental dimensions of our immediate experience. When dealing with my shoulder pain, "It hurts me," then becomes "I am hurting."

Focus on an emotional problem in which you are stuck. Think through all the alternative choices that you may have -- giving up, getting angry, running away. List the advantages and disadvantages of each and "rationally" choose one as best for you. Notice how you feel. Now take a few deep breaths and allow your consciousness to go to that part of your body where you hold on to your problem -- tightened diaphragm, aching back, headache, hunched shoulders, etc. Stay with the feeling in this part of your body. Allow the feeling to increase, while you exaggerate the body position.
Become this part of your body by saying "I am my diaphragm" or "back," etc. Let yourself continue to speak as this part of your body,

expressing as directly and fully as you can all that is happening. Relax and take a few breaths. Notice how you feel. Is your feeling now different? List the choices with advantages and disadvantages? Is your choice the same? Do you have a different feeling about your choice?

All aspects of me are simultaneously present. I am not now my body, later having an effect on my mind. If any dimension or aspect of my experience is being modified, every other aspect of me is also being modified, because all of me is now present in a single unity. That is not to say that one part of me is presently acting on another part; for example, that the release of tension in my muscles is causing a corresponding release in my emotions and thoughts. Rather, the release of my physical tension **is** the release of my emotional and mental frustration. And conversely, the release of these frustrations **is** the release of my physical tension.

This discussion may seem abstract and philosophical, but I feel it can be helpful for understanding in the following chapters the way in which I work with individuals. Bodymind is a single phenomenon, which we experience as a stream of moments or events. I do not consider these events to be separable into independent physical sensations, emotions, thoughts, or any similar traditional contents of consciousness. My experience is singular and undivided. Of course, I may focus on some aspect of this experience, but every other aspect is still functioning along with the parts to which I am presently giving attention. Let me illustrate. The pain I am now feeling in my back is a functional property of my bodymind, but so too are my fear and doubting attitude. All of these -- pain, fear, doubt -- although they can be described separately as physical, emotional, and mental, are a single stream of experience.

When I direct my attention toward my "body" or "mind," I do not isolate one from the other. I am merely focusing in the foreground of my experience one moment of my unified bodymind, allowing other simultaneous aspects of bodymind to stay in the background. Don Johnson in **The Protean Body** expresses this view of bodymind less philosophically and more poetically when he writes:

> The person is like a plant whose fibrils, nearly indistinguishable from their nourishing soil, flow into the roots that flow into the trunk that differentiates into branches and leaves and flowers and beyond into the electrical field surrounding it. Spiritual consciousness, emotions and feelings, intelligence, physiochemical functioning, the musculoskeletal systems, are all only viewpoints from which we can examine the single reality we are.(3)

This view of human experience can also be seen in some models of physiological functioning. The classical theory of the production of pain is that stimuli act on specific pain receptors in the skin and travel along a message center to a pain center in the brain.(4) An alternative, and I believe more workable view, derived from current neurophysiological data, is that pain is not a response but rather a phenomenon which consists of both outer stimuli and inner activity and which flows through a system of opening and closing gates in the nervous system.(5) Ronald Melzack writes, "...sensory mechanisms alone fail to account for pain. We (Melzack and Wall) propose that the presence or absence of pain is determined by the balance between the sensory and the central inputs to the gate-control system."(6) We shall see in later chapters that this model can help us understand the experience of letting go of our accumulated armor.

A similar example of unified bodymind action is the model of myofascial functioning described by Ida Rolf, the acknowledged pioneer in the field of deep tissue bodywork. She stated:

> If the myofascial system is considered as a functional whole rather than as a merely additive complex of tissue, it becomes apparent that this is the organ of support -- a resilient unitary fascial framework which initiates, transmits, and

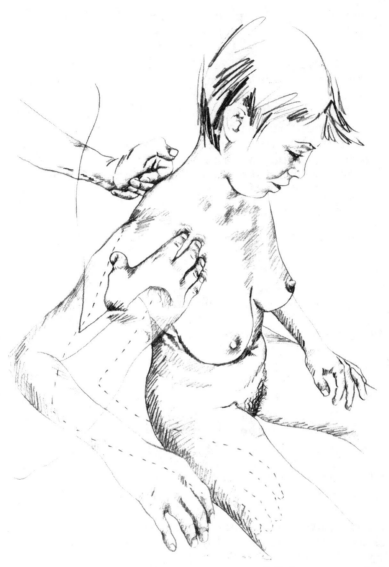

Deep bodywork can help a person establish an easy balance between different muscle groups. Often when we move an arm, we unconsciously overstretch muscles in the middle of the back, (the lower rhomboids), which help to hold the scapulae and shoulders in place. When this happens the opposing muscles on the front of the body (e.g., pectoralis minor) are overcontracted, and as the arm moves forward, so does the shoulder. Here the practitioner is working simultaneously on the rhomboids in back and the pectoralis minor in front, encouraging the client to move his arm from the elbow, while keeping the shoulder stable.

determines movement, as well as ensheathing and supporting all individual parts.(7)

She carried this model even further when she said:

> Emotional response is behavior, is function. All behavior is expressed through the musculoskeletal system. All function is an expression of structure and form correlates directly with material structure. A man crying the blues is in reality bewailing his structural limitations and failures.(8)

In this passage she, in effect, made emotion a functional aspect of the physical person. She seemed, however, unwilling to give emotion (and presumably also cognition) equal status with the body. She treated body structure or function as the underlying cause of emotional functions.

In a discourse concerning a chronically angry individual she wrote:

> Until the physical situation can somehow be changed, the psychotherapist can make very little headway. "You do not run because you are afraid, you are afraid because you run," said William James at the turn of this century, and nothing since has changed the validity of his observation. Our angry friend is chronically angry because his body is still fixed in a physical attitude of anger.(9)

It seems to me that she here assigned emotion (and perhaps thought as well) to the role of an "epi-phenomenon," a kind of activity which is caused by, or emerges out of physical functioning. As such, emotion and mind are still a product, however complicated, of the body, and what we have, I believe, is a subtle materialism which finally reduces mind to body.

I believe that the view I am proposing is closer to a true monism, the belief that body and mind are one reality, one single kind of functioning stuff. I see the body as much a functional mirror of emotion (and thought) as emotion is a mirror of body. We can no more explain the mind in terms of the body, than we can explain the body in terms of the mind. But we can explain both as equal aspects of the same dynamic reality.

In his informative and useful book, **Bodymind,** Ken Dychwald writes about Rolfing, the generic name usually given to the Ida Rolf form of deep bodywork:

> **New awareness ... comes only with an alteration in being, feeling, thinking, and believing. So, then, it would seem that unless there is a corresponding change in the habits and attitudes that create body shape, purely physical manipulations of the body are left without a new mental structure in which to take root. For this reason, I feel that Rolfing is partly deficient as a complete bodywork process, as it does not allow people to experience themselves and the changes that are possible within their own bodyminds slowly and mindfully. It is too much a matter of something that someone does "to" you, rather than something you consciously do yourself.(10)**

I endorse the general spirit of this observation. My view differs slightly in that, for me, mental structure is not something in which the body can take root; no more than mind can take root in the body. Body and mind have no separate structural or causal properties in the first place. When we deal with body we are already dealing with mind and vice versa.

We can deceive ourselves by trying to deal with the body as the causal support of mind or to deal with mind as the supporting structure which creates body. But I see the actual gradual changes which are brought about in bodywork as the changes which occur from one unified moment of bodymind to the next unified moment. Body or mind, if treated separately -- now with body techniques, or now with emotive or cognitive therapies -- shows little change, and the armor merely reappears in a new form.

As we shall see in the following chapters, true transformation is a change of our total being and can occur through the help of a practitioner using simultaneously a variety of techniques -- deep tissue release, breathwork, emotional expression, movement awareness.

INSIDE AND OUTSIDE
The Melting of Core and Shell

When lasting change does occur, it is, in one sense, instantaneous and complete. As my body is changing, my mind is also changing, for they are both functions of the same immediate experience. In some aspects of my whole bodymind I am immediately freer. Not only does my body move more easily, my feelings and thoughts are also more flowing. But I still have more bodymind armor to get rid of. I may, for example, become emotionally and mentally clear about the anger I have locked in my forearms, but continue to repress and keep unconscious the sadness in my sunken chest. Just as I gradually developed my armor I can also gradually dissolve it.

Before we turn to this process in the next chapter, we need first to look at how armor can gradually develop, how we very early in our lives create a kind of inner resistance, or "core," and around it create an outer protection or "shell."

We have already seen how our development is a history of learned responses, many of which we turn into rigid habits for protecting us against pain, but which also prevent our completeness and spontaneity. The earliest of these habits form the core of resistance. During the trauma we experience at the moment of conception, while moving along the fallopian tubes, and when implanting and gestating in the uterus, we are that early in our existence already establishing patterns for handling the world and protecting ourselves. We reinforce this developing, protective core as we are forced to cope with the shock of birth, and to then struggle through the oral, anal, and genital phases of our infantile growth. By the age of three or four years, we have almost fully developed our characteristic postures, our ways of avoiding pain and unwanted change.

The rest of our lives is usually a reinforcement of this core, years of similarly accumulated, protective responses. But we make our armor even more complicated by creating more protection, a veneer placed around the core. For although the core is the most resistent part of us, it is also the most vulnerable to intense pain. The shell may allow us to take some risks. If we get hurt there, it is superficial, and we are still protected at the deeper level.

We maintain this basic division between core and shell in many forms. Sometimes, as we shall see in later discussing bodymind types, the body itself can reveal a hard exterior of overdeveloped extrinsic muscles (for locomotion), covering a center of weak, intrinsic muscles (for balance). As an example, consider the muscle-bound athlete, who has temporary strength but no grace. Conversely, the outside can be a soft physical buffer around a tight but passive center. Look at the "delicate" feminine type woman who is "hard as nails" under the surface. This separation into outside shell and inside core also happens at the emotional and cognitive levels. Our everyday social feelings may be flat and controlled, yet cover deeper explosive emotions. Or if we are gregarious, we may, nonetheless, hold back inner feelings of doubt and fear.

When we divide ourselves into an outside shell and inside core, we create a frustrating illusion that the two cannot function together. R. D. Laing in Knots poignantly expresses the riddle of that struggle with the following lines:

> One is inside
> then outside what one has been inside
> one feels empty
> because there is nothing inside oneself
> one tries to get inside oneself
> that inside of the outside
> that one was once inside
> once one tries to get oneself inside what
> one is outside...(11)

The alternative to this armored splitting of ourselves into a core and shell is to move, to feel, to think with our

SELF-HELP EXERCISE #2

Sit upright in a chair with your feet and legs straight ahead. Take a deep breath and notice how easy or difficult it is for you to flow easily between the diaphragm and upper chest and throat. Feel the muscles of your chest and throat and notice any tension restricting your breathing.

After preparing yourself with several minutes of deep breathing reach under your ribcage on both sides with your fingers and hands. As you very slowly roll your spine forward into your hands, exhale and let your movement push your hands further under the cage. As your hands go deeper into the tissue press with your fingers against the inside wall of your rib cage. Stop your rolling movement and inhale, easing your pressure. Again exhale and continue your movement and pressure. When you reach a position as far forward as possible inhale, so that your diaphragm descends and pushes down against your fingers.

While in this position you may notice a tightness or choking sensation in the throat. Softly but deliberately cough, keeping your hands under your ribs. Stay with any feelings which may surface. Often when we swallow our feelings (by constricting our throats) we are also holding onto our abdominal (diaphragmatic) breathing. We are literally squeezing ourselves with bands of armor, around the throat, and around the lower rib cage.

Relax and slowly roll back to an upright sitting position. Take a deep breath and see if an inner release has freed your breathing, helping you feel more connected from the throat to the diaphragm. Check to see if the muscles around your chest are softer.

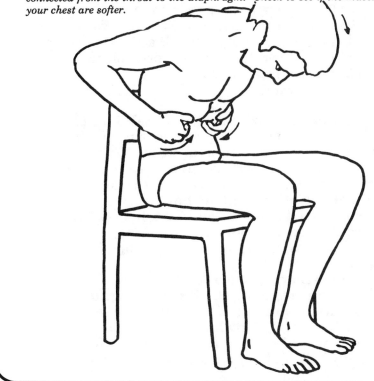

whole being, letting what is happening in our outside life be what is happening in our inside life. When we are most alive, that is, fully responsive to our environment, as well as active in it, our energy is not limited to surface reactions or inner initiatives. Fear, anger, joy, sympathy, and grief move freely through us, from the outward contact with the people around us, pouring right into our deeper feelings of empathy and sharing. At the same time, those emotions can begin inside us and without repression flow outward toward others. Thus when we are fully alive, the core and shell both disintegrate, and our energy moves easily from outside to inside and from inside to outside.

Reaction and action are different views of the same event. My reaction to you is a mode of my action toward you. When you touch me, my response is my active acceptance or rejection of you. My inside and outside energetically function together as aspects of my single unified reality. This unity can be felt in the body tissue. When there is unity, there is balance between the larger intrinsic muscles (which give power to our movement) and the deeper intrinsic muscles (which give subtle direction and stability). The unarmored, active and receptive individual has a consistent, soft yet firm tone from the skin inward to the deepest structures.

Try the following exercises:

At the side of a swimming pool fall into the water, bracing yourself tensely against any stinging pain you feel on splashing into the water. Try again, this time relaxing and letting out a yell as you feel impact with the surface. Compare the two experiences. Notice that although you were defending yourself the first time, the pain may have been less the second, more relaxed time, as you allowed it to pass through you and be completely expressed.

Have a partner surprise you by screaming or shouting at you several times without giving notice. React as fully as you can. How complete can you make your response? Now have your partner call out the names of different emotions -- "fear," "anger," "joy," etc. Act out each of these as quickly

**and completely as you can. After several times do
you find it easier to initiate and completely express
an emotion?**

Practitioners of some types of bodywork emphasize the
importance of working with the outer defenses (the shell)
before going to deeper levels of resistance at the core. In
these approaches, as I mentioned in the previous chapter,
it is as if layers of the body, much like the layers of an
onion, are peeled away one at a time. These bodyworkers
seem to believe that before a person can reveal and express
the innermost blocks, he or she must first let go of the more
superficial outside armor.

As I shall explain in the next chapter, in wholistic
bodywork, the practitioner works gradually in two
directions: from the shell toward the core, and at the same
time from the core toward the shell. When attending to
both these directions, we also can respect the need, at any
given stage, for focusing part of our work on a certain
depth of release. For example, while concentrating on
superficial fascia, I will at the same time use strokes
which begin the release of deep structures, and while
concentrating on deep fascia, I simultaneously rework
superficial layers to insure the completeness and evenness
of the release.

Let us turn now to the actual process and experience of
releasing our armor.

FOOTNOTES FOR CHAPTER II

1. **The Body and Mature Behavior,** M. Feldenkrais
    (New York: International Universities Press, 1973)
    p.53.
2. See Both:
    Wilhelm Reich, by David Boadella (New York, Dell-
    Laurel, 1975). Also: **Orgone, Reich, and Eros,** W.E.
    Mann (New York: Simon and Shuster, 1973).

3. **The Protean Body**, Don Johnson (New York: Harper and Row,   1977) p.21.
4. **The Puzzle of Pain**, Ronald Melzack (New York: Basic Books, 1973) p.126.
5. **Ibid.**, pp. 168-190.
6. **Ibid.**, p.171.
7. "Structural Integration: A contribution to the Understanding of Stress," Ida Rolf, **Confinia Psychiatrica** XVI (1973): 71.
8. **Rolfing, The Integration of Human Structures** Ida Rolf (Santa Monica: Dennis Landman, 1977) p.17.
9. **Ibid.**, pp.26-27.
10. **Bodymind**, Ken Dychwald (New York: Jove Books, 1977) p.127.
11. **Knots**, R.D. Lang (Middlesex: Penguin, 1970) p.83.

CHAPTER III

THE PROCESS AND EXPERIENCE OF RELEASE

You may at times have felt that you were finally beginning to make some progress with your problems, that after being stuck a long time, you seemed suddenly to find your plans working and to have reasons to be optimistic about the future. Then, just as suddenly you may have found yourself stuck again, having the same fantasies of what you wanted for yourself, but unable to fulfill them.

When our consciousness of ourselves -- of our bodies, of our abilities, of our needs -- is out of tune with reality, we easily mistake our superficial changes for a deeper fulfillment. Our consciousness reflects the confusion and incompleteness of our bodies. We may have a very needy body, restricted and lacking in strength and yet we may have fantasies of doing all kinds of things which require more power than we really have. We, then, easily confuse the excitement of newness with what would really be helpful and nourishing.

Try the following:

Borrow a car from your neighbor which is either much smaller or much larger than your own. Notice as you park or drive on the road how difficult it is to judge the space you have on the opposite side of the car and in front and back. Notice how and where you are not fully aware of your own body. Notice that chronic pains or even the symptoms of illness are in parts which you have not totally accepted into your consciousness.

Now focus on that part of your body where you frequently have discomfort or pain, or where you feel weak or unconscious. Be this part of your body and express what is happening, e.g, the lower leg can say, "Jack give me more attention don't just stand on me; rest me, massage me, take care of me"

In order to change at a deeper, more permanent level of bodymind we need a way of discovering the discrepancy between what we superficially "think" we need and what is actually possible, helpful, and satisfying. We need to let go of our fantasies of ourselves and begin to settle more into the real self.

Postural Integration is just such a process. By directly working with the body we feel and define its limits, and at the same time we are finding the limits of our fantasies. As we open the tensions restricting our bodies we may be less interested in busy projects and more centered in our need to take care of ourselves and build our strength. This is a gradual process, a process of letting go of the past and exploring new possibilities in the present moment. Gradually we sink into ourselves and discover our wholeness.

Although there are many approaches to deep bodywork (to the extent it respects the three principles which I outlined in Chapter I -- unity, balance, and shared interaction) Postural Integration is one of the most effective, because its results are tangible, rapid, and lasting. (Examine the before and after photographs near the end of Chapter V).

At the end of each session one can observe tactile and visible changes, and these changes accumulate with each additional session. But there is more than these tangible changes: there is an unfolding experience, a developing understanding of what it is to let go of our defenses and open to new possibilities. In this chapter I want first to describe for you the steps involved in releasing armor and second to share with you how I understand the experience of this release.

Of course there is more to permanent change than just releasing and understanding our old blocks. We need also to integrate this new found freedom into ourselves so that we are centered and stable in our movements and feelings. In the next chapter I am going to look at how we can, while changing, be grounded and centered.

The work, therefore, progresses in two general stages: the release of armor and the integration of this release. Of course, in both stages we are concerned with the whole bodymind, with all attendant sensations, feelings, thoughts, and beliefs, but in describing this process it is often easier, for purposes of identifying the steps, to focus on parts of the physical body.

The first stage, concentrating on release, consists of four phases:

1) The initial opening of armored structures, usually given in two sessions, one session on the top half of the body and one on the bottom half;

2) Lateral elongation between the torso and pelvis,a slightly deeper, intermediate level of work;

3) Pelvic release, three sessions of very deep work on the inside of the thighs, the inner abdomen, and the structure lying beneath the outer buttocks;

4) Release of head and neck armor in which the neck is softened from inside the mouth.

The second stage, integration, to be treated in the next chapter, consists of three sessions of reorganizing and balancing the entire bodymind, sessions which help harmonize the top-bottom, front-back, and left-right relationships of the complete structure.

I have clearly been influenced in developing this sequence by my experience and observation of Rolfing. In 1969, Bill Williams, who has since developed his own form of wholistic work called "Soma," helped me through more than twenty sessions of Rolfing. (I also received some sessions from Ida Rolf). I experienced many important changes because of Bill's sensitivity, but as I recounted in the Prologue, the traditional Rolfing sequence left me feeling incomplete. I find its sequence of sessions too rigid, not only with respect to the order in which body segments are handled, but also with respect to the single direction in which it progresses from outer to inner layers of the body and to the lack of attention given emotional and mental change.

I have outlined Postural Integration as a process normally consisting of five phases with a total of ten sessions. Each phase may actually require more sessions than I have indicated. There may be a great mass of accumulated emotional and mental armor to be released and when the tissue is very resistant, additional sessions

THE PROCESS OF RELEASE AND INTEGRATION

	SEGMENTS AND MUSCULATURE	FASCIAE	ATTITUDES, MOVEMENTS, FEELINGS
FIRST STAGE: Release of Armor in Individual Bodymind Segments			
PHASE I: Initial Opening of Bodymind Armor	Balancing the outside: upper and lower structures		
SESSION 1: Upper Half	Thorax, arms, lateral hips, iliotibial tract, ischia, neck, dorsal and lumbar spine	Superficial envelop	Surface feelings, momentary reactions, habitual defenses
SESSION 2: Lower Half	Feet, ankles, lower legs, knees, hamstrings, connections to upper half	Superficial pectoralis, abdominus, capitae, colli, nuchae, axillaris, extremitatis superioris	Feelings of being energized or relieved
		Superficial extremitatis inferior	Memories of childhood mobility and freedom, grounding, attitudes toward parents
PHASE II: Elongation	Distance between pelvis and cage, shaping (ovality) of thorax, placement of shoulders	Intermediate fascia, superficial part of deep envelopes	Vulnerability along the flanks
SESSION 3: Hips to Shoulders	Hips, cage, shoulders & neck, quad lumborum, lat dorsi, rotators of arms, trapezius	Profunda: dorsi, lumbodorsalis, axillaris, scapulae, nuchae	Increased consciousness in back, lateral mobility enhanced
PHASE III: Pelvic Reorientation	Bottom and front of lower pelvis, top of pelvis and abdomen, back of pelvis and lower back	Deep envelopes around and inside of pelvis	Discovery of central balance, hara consciousness
SESSION 4: Lower Pelvis	Inside of thighs, adductors, front of thighs, rectus femoris, sartorius	Deepest envelopes of adductors, full release of fascia lata	Opening and widening of ischia, lengthening in front, confrontation with sexual feelings
SESSION 5: Upper Pelvis	Abdominus rectus, chest, diaphragm, obliques, psoas	Profunda: scarpa, transversalis, pelvia; envelopes and attachments of ilio-psoas	Settling of abdominal contents into pelvic bowl; joy, sadness, sexual mobility
SESSION 6: Back of Pelvis	Hamstrings, gluteals, rotators, sacrum, sacrospinalis, coccyx	Profunda: lata, pelvia dorsi, envelopes of piriformis, gemelli; obturators, quadratus femoris	Anal anger, male fear of homosexuality, extroverted energy
PHASE IV: Release of Neck And Head			
SESSION 7: Neck and Head	Clavicle, thoracic inlet, neck, scalp, jaw, mouth, tongue, cheeks, nose, eyes	Profunda: nuchae, colli, capitis	Primitive emotions of face, deep pain and release; increase in range of rotation of head
SECOND STAGE: Integration Of All Parts And Aspects Of Bodymind	Connecting segments	All layers move simultaneously	New balance, feeling of wholeness, flowing of emotions and thoughts
PHASE V: Coordinating Upper And Lower Halves	Coordination of either lower or upper segments with each other	Planes of fasciae on opposite half are opened	Feeling of deep opening toward the top or bottom
SESSION 8: Usually Lower Half	Freeing of pelvis and lower extremities	Lifting and lengthening fascia of trunk out of pelvic bowl as result of work on lower half	Feeling that grounding and consciousness in lower half are necessary to freedom above
SESSION 9: Usually Upper Half	Expansion of trunk and upper extremities	Expansion of diaphragmatic fascia downward and outward	Feeling that expression of freedom and needs in upper body helps grounding
SESSION 10: Overall Reorganization	Coordination and connection from front to back and left to right	Freedom and interplay of all fascial layers	Feeling of completeness; front-back, and left-right balance

68

may also be needed. In any case, it is important that there is sufficient release during one phase before going on to the next phase.

Up to this point I have emphasized that the release of armor (and the integration of new energy) is a process of unravelling (and harmonizing) our bodies and minds together, as well as our inside and outside selves. However, release (and integration) is also the relaxation of excessive muscular contractions and the establishing of a physiological balance between opposing muscles. In any part of the body, when one group of muscles functions as the force moving a part of our skeleton in one direction, an opposing group of muscles moves this part of our skeleton in the opposite direction. Take, for example, the movement of the lower leg. The hamstring muscles are powerful flexors, as when we lift the heel toward the buttocks, while the muscles on the front of the thigh are extensors and straighten the leg.

These opposing groups of muscles (flexors and extensors, adductors and abductors, supinators and pronators, medial and lateral rotators) maintain the front-back, top-bottom, and left- right positioning of the body via their equalizing contractions. But as we armor ourselves by developing habitual attitudes, some of the opposing groups become overcontracted and thereby create postural imbalances. The person with rounded shoulders is "out of front-back balance," and is overcontracting the pectoralis minor, a small, deep muscle, attached to the front of the shoulder. At the same time, the lower and upper rhomboids, muscles which pull the shoulders backward, are undercontracted.

When we create such an imbalance between two groups of muscles in one part of the body, we have to compensate with an imbalance, an overcontraction, in the other direction, in another part of the body, otherwise we could not remain upright. When I round my shoulders, I would topple forward if I did not overcontract the muscles of my lower back. The body is a marvel of zigzagging contractions, holding us upright, even though we stubbornly hold on to the strains in each part of us.

I previously mentioned in Chapter II how fascia envelopes our muscles and is the mechanism for guiding and coordinating movement. When some groups of our muscles are overcontracted the surrounding fascia has shortened and thickened, making the imbalance chronic. The person with rounded shoulders will have layers of hardened, immobile fascia covering the front of the shoulder and chest which prevents enough relaxation for the muscles between the shoulder blades to exert an opposing force and pull the shoulders back.

There are, of course, also those cases of overcontraction where a person seems to be upright and in balance. The opposing muscles groups may be in balance, for example those holding the pelvis in alignment, but both groups are overcontracted. This is not true balance, but rigidity, which will eventually break down the structure of the body. We see this in weightlifters and dancers who have forced their bodies into alignment but who, as they grow older, become stiffer and less flexible.

When the muscle groups are in an easy balance with each other, the tension of the body is evenly distributed throughout the fascial network. The body can then lengthen, taking weight off the bones and allowing them to function along parallel lines which run through a series of horizontally arranged hinges or axes. In this model of gravitational efficiency the feet work best straight ahead, along two parallel lines running through the middle of the legs. On these two lines there are horizontal hinges which allow the body to easily bend along its parallel tracks: the metatarsal hinge at the foot, the ankle hinge, and the knee hinge.

Broader hinges span the pelvis and upper body: the sacro-femoral hinge at the pelvis, the lumbo-dorsal hinge at the hara, the mid-thoracic hinge running through the chest and shoulder blades, and the cervical hinge in the neck. These upper axes work along parallel lines which run from the sitbones (ischia) through the eyes, and from the inside of the thighs (lesser trochanters) through the ears. You can easily understand how bunching and thickening of the fascial planes skews these hinges, tilting and twisting them into inefficient patterns. This is, of course, a gravitational model, a rather ideal model, of how a body might function.

70

The following images may help you better understand this model:

Parallel Lines. Imagine the body as organized along two parallel lines. When the legs are turned in or out or if they are spread too wide or too narrow, the body cannot move efficiently along these straight ahead rails.

Right Angle Axes. Imagine that the body functions by means of a series of axes at right angles to these parallel lines. These axes pass through the joints at the toes, ankles, knees, pelvis, mid-thorax, and head. If these axes are tilted away from right angles, the body alignment moves from side to side.

Stacked Blocks. Imagine a vertical line which passes through the ankle, pelvis, mid-lateral thorax, and ear. If this line is tilted forward or backward, the segments of the body can no longer stack one on top of the other. The image of a dragon tail can help bring the pelvis from a swayed position into easy alignment. The image of the thorax opening evenly outward like an umbrella helps make the cage rounder and more balanced. The image of a string lifting from the crown of the head allows a chin which is lifted too high to drop down.

This model does not easily account for the emotional and mental aspects of our lives and we cannot force bodymind into such a mold. But it helps us begin to see possible ways that basic parts of the body can work in harmony with each other. In later chapters I want to return to this question of how much we need to respect the limits of bodymind and not try to force individuals into models or categories which work counter to the natural flow of their energy.

Looking at the body more anatomically, I am dividing the fascia into three layers, the superficial, the intermediate, and deep. My use of these designations does not correspond to any one system of anatomical classification but is a mixture of ideas taken from German, French, and English anatomical texts.(1) What I call "superficial" comprises both the fatty and denser subcutaneous layers. What I call "intermediate" is referred to in some texts as the "superficial subserous fascia," and what I call "deep" as the "deep subserous fascia." More simply, right under the skin we find the superficial fascia, at the tops of the muscular envelopes the intermediate fascia, and around the muscles and at their attachments the deep fascia.

In working with these layers of fascia I want to soften and reorganize them. Sheets of fascia have a tendency to thicken and adhere to surrounding tissues. An important part of the process is to separate these sheets of fascia such that muscle fiber can soften and function more freely. In the separating and softening process I pay attention to the depth of my strokes. In the accompanying diagrams you will see that depth is controlled by the angle at which I apply force with fingers, fists, etc. Depth is also to a certain extent controlled by the amount of force I use.

I want also to encourage the coordination of different parts of the fascial system. In superficial work I am working with flat broad strokes toward a spreading of the outer envelope around the whole body -- a general, spacious, fluffing out of the whole subcutaneous layer. In intermediate work I go slightly deeper with shorter strokes and begin touching and opening individual myofascial envelopes, the wrappings around individual muscles. In deep work I go in between and under envelopes, and the strokes are very slow and short. As we shall see in later chapters, during the integrating of fascial planes, which is possible only after deep release of the envelopes, I often work with two hands, spanning and harmonizing the length and width of large segments of tissue.

Paying attention to these layers, practitioners of deep bodywork -- using fingers, fists, knuckles, and elbows -- release the hardened fascia, which holds muscular overcontractions. Using careful, sytematic manipulations, and coordinating the release of outer layers and inner layers, they simultaneously work with emotional and mental aspects of bodymind.

PHASE I: INITIAL RELEASE

Inspiration and New Direction

At the beginning of this chapter I spoke of how our fantasies may go beyond our real power. But our fantasies also often hold us back from what we are really capable. I may have fantastic ideas about my sexual abilities; on the other hand when I surrender my macho pride I may be more tender than I or my friends thought possible. Change initiates new possibilities.

The first phase of the process is an initiation into a new process. By moving the superficial tissue a new dimension of feelings, thoughts, and movements becomes possible. As my body begins to open, to take more space, my attitudes break free from their old molds. Take for example the young man who has always been very skinny. In trying to change himself he has always thought that he must build up his body with exercise and more food intake. But when he exercises and eats more, he becomes more active, tighter, but loses weight. His attitude has been one of extreme neediness but resignation to never being able to satisfy himself. After two sessions of Postural Integration without doing anything he rapidly begins to gain weight. His muscles get fuller but less tense. He is excited in feeling he can change by not trying but by simply feeling his own capacity to give to himself.

The first phase inspires us by showing us that we are changing in a way we did not really see or understand. This happens through an opening of the protective shell of superficial fascia with which we have surrounded ourselves. But at the same time, as this shell moves and becomes responsive, we are also beginning, deep inside us, to realize that there are new ways in which we can reshape ourselves.

Superficial fascia is a thin envelope that stretches over the whole body just beneath the skin. When free and even in its function, it lubricates, guides and supports the body mass. Some individuals, in an attempt to protect them-

73

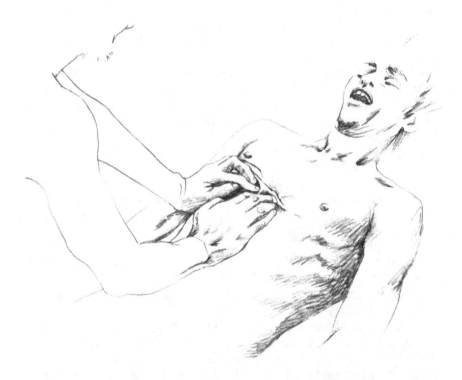

During the first phase, the practitioner hooks just beneath the surface of the skin and frees the superficial fascia, a thin envelope that stretches over the whole body, and which, when free in its function, lubricates, guides, and supports the body's mass.

selves from the "hard knocks" of life, turn this thin envelope into a kind of "thick skin," which then adheres to underlying structures. Others develop a different kind of buffer, a rubbery superficial layer which is flaccid and relatively unresponsive to the touch. These persons armor themselves by passively letting the outer tissue absorb the stress, while tightening inside. In Chapter VI I will discuss the different degrees and arrangements of tension which constitute several basic character or bodymind types.

When working with this superficial armor, I use my fingers to hook carefully just the outer sleeve of the body, and also to coordinate this outer movement with deep inner transformation, as seen in the following example.

Zelda, from a peasant family, grew up outside Zurich with eight brothers. As an active tomboy she had always considered herself equal to her brothers in strength and agility, but in so doing she swallowed her feelings of being inadequate as a girl. Her musculature was well defined, and the surface tissue was so tightly drawn over her rib cage that I was unable to hook into and move the superficial envelope.

With one hand I continued to attempt to hook onto the superficial tissue, while at the same time I placed the fingers of my other hand deep in her throat. At first there was no reaction at all, then as her whole body pulsed from a series of gag reflexes, I felt the tissue of her chest begin to move. She then shared with me how she had felt weak inside and unable to show her feminine side during her childhood. Her outer structure responded only as her inner structure, through her feelings, became active.

Often in this first stage of work with my clients, I work with a variety of deep inner reactions and structures, e.g., around the base of the tongue where we hold the messages of our hearts (we need to speak with our hearts), inside the nose in order to elicit the sadness we store in our eyes, and around the anus to help us confront our anger against

75

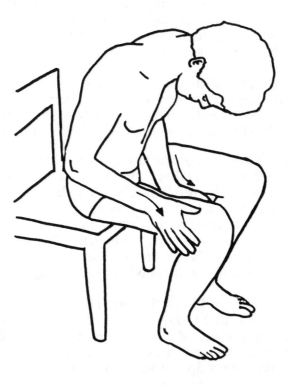

Sit in a chair with your feet on the floor. Place the heels of both hands on your right or left front thigh, halfway between the knee and the groin. Lean forward onto both hands and with equal force use hooking movements to spread the tissue in opposite directions. You must use the weight of your upper body and wait for the tissue to relax, allowing a spreading of structures just under the skin. The sensation is often hot, even slightly uncomfortable, yet releasing of deep tension.

authority. These inner releases, when coordinated with superficial strokes promote a gradual, even, and lasting unfolding of the self simultaneously from inside toward the outside as well as the outside toward the inside.

I have found it natural that lasting change cannot be limited to a part of us. If I am truly open to you, even if we are only encountering each other in our exterior lives, I have in some way already contacted you more deeply. In wholistic bodywork we are respecting how gradual and progressive our work needs to be. If I try too soon or too persistently to open totally the core, the result may be confusion and even greater armoring against becoming more open; or if I remain only at a superficial level, if I hesitate to go to the core of my client, the changes will be temporary and the resistance will eventually manifest itself in a new form.

The first phase, then, is concentrated on the whole superficial envelope. I usually divide the work into one session on the upper half of the body, and one session on the lower half.

The big superficial covering around the thorax is like a shopping bag or sweater which is weak in some places and crimped together in others. Often the symptoms of this unevenness show up at the weaker spots -- the belly dumps over the pelvic basin, the shoulder blades fall apart and are pulled forward. But it is in the tight areas that one can best begin reorganizing. When we smooth out or fluff out thickened clumps of fascia, we promote a spreading and consistency along the entire fascial plane, taking stress off weaker areas, and at the same time giving space for inner structures to rearrange themselves, e.g., the bladder settles under the intestines, instead of behind it, as in the case of a protunding belly (pytosis).

This is an example of the principle: work where the symptom is not. A principle which can apply at the emotional and mental levels as well. If we move around (do not always directly confront) our emotional frustrations, we can often find other emotions and attitudes which are easier to express and which will help us, eventually, return to, and work through, the original problem.

The chest is often blocked at the mid-thoracic hinge, an imaginary axis, running right through the thorax, which

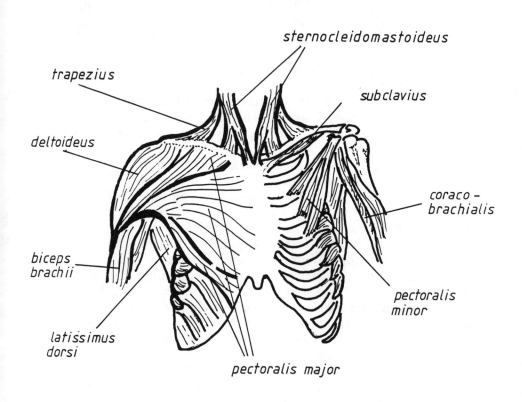

trapezius

sternocleidomastoideus

deltoideus

subclavius

coraco-
brachialis

biceps
brachii

latissimus
dorsi

pectoralis
minor

pectoralis major

allows us to flex and extend part of the upper rib cage and spine. But a line of tension, running around the middle of the chest, often blocks the capacity of the ribs and spine to bend. Imagine a belt pulled so tight it squeezes the ribs and breasts together. First of all, this band of armor can cut off the coordination between the breath in the upper chest and abdomen, such that one breathes in only one half. We may be puffed-out and overcharged in the upper chest, while not allowing any breath or feeling below. On the other hand, we may fill the abdomen but neglect to breathe high enough to claim the power in our upper chest and throat.

I work with this split by reaching under the ribs at the costal arch, by lifting the superficial tissue upward on the front of the chest, by opening the seam of thickened tissue along the sternum, and by pulling the hard, depressed tissue (on top of the platysma) over the clavicle and around the sides of the neck.

Second, if we follow this band of armor around the chest to the middle of the back, we find a related confusion in the lower rhomboids, which when functioning smoothly, gently hold and guide our shoulders at the mid-thoracic hinge. When the chest is collapsed in front (with an overcontraction of the pectoralis minor), the rhomboids are slack and the shoulder blades drift forward.

This confusion is also evident when the chest is high and the shoulders pulled back. The shoulder blades may be held together above the mid-thoracic hinge by the upper rhomboid muscles and yet the lower rhomboids may remain slack. I work with this confusion by working over and down the shoulder (trapezius and levator scapula), by working to release the upper rhomboids, and by broadening and lengthening the lower back.

These movements (upward in front and downward in the back), by bringing together separated parts of the thorax, create a flowing, vibrating breath and feelings of both surrender and power. But it is not only the cage which needs to be better connected within itself. We also cut off other parts of ourselves as well. The arms may hang listless at the sides, or be overcontracted in eagerness and anger. The hips need to move with the diaphragm as it expands toward the sides and back, but they may remain frozen and immobile.

79

This latter problem between the diaphragm and hips is part of a band of armor which often extends around the body along the lumbo-dorsal hinge. This hinge gets stuck in a forward tilting position, giving us a sway back. I use broad strokes with both hands moving in opposite directions, one hand upward along the superficial thoracic tissue, the other downward across the gluteal tissue of the hip. While making such bidirectional strokes I ask my clients to let their breath travel down and back -- which begins to rock the pelvis -- until one can see that the breath goes not only to the twelveth rib, but downward through the pelvis and even into the legs. When the breath is "lowered" in this way, we can begin to focus less on overstriving and pride found in narrow, high, anterior breathing, and settle back into a more grounded, patient attitude.

Connecting the thorax with the arms is equally important, since many of our habitual movements of the arms needlessly also activate muscles of the upper chest. When we flex the lower arm with the biceps, we may also pull the shoulder blades forward with the pectoralis minor. The function of the two muscles is confused and a thickening may begin to occur in the tissues stretching between the chest and upper arm, and the arm will be chronically stuck in a forward position. Again bidirectional strokes with both hands (between the chest and arm) will help create more space for the arm to fall back into place, giving more space to the joining of the arm and shoulder (glenoid cavity).

After working in one session on the upper half of the body, a remarkable thing happens. The client begins to feel lighter and taller, yet the legs may be a little stiffer or more confused in their movements. This is a positive sign. Large sections of tissue have become more elastic and fluid, but since they are only one part of a very long and broad sheet, the other end, the lower half, begins to contract with some of this shifting tension.

The legs are our contact with that very early part of ourselves with which, hesitant or confident, we took initial steps toward our parents. The ankles are one of the keys to this basic grounding.

At the ankles we often find that the horizontal axis running through the two ankle bones (internal and external malleoli), is tilted in or out. Tilting in gives us flat feet and often expresses our immaturity, our unwillingness to take responsibility, to respond to the earth with a firm, contracting medial arch. Here the problem lies on the lateral side of the leg, where powerful muscles (peroneals) are turning (everting) the foot inward. The long thin bone which guides this action, the fibula, is confused, its lower shaft probably rotated inward (medial) and forward.

The strategy is to work across the fibula on the outside of the lower leg and give more space for the peroneals to relax. This strategy will, in turn, allow the antagonistic muscles on the inside of the leg (e.g. tibialis posterior) to contract and lift the arch. Of course the medial arch can be too independent, too high. The foot needs to have the capacity to flatten out, to spread out on the ground, but then contract and lift us as we shift our weight onto the foot.

In order to get the foot to flatten out, we release not just the high inner arch. In fact there are three arches: what we usually designate on the inside is the medial arch; there is the transverse arch or instep, and along the outside of the foot we find the lateral. When the foot flattens and then responds, all three of these arches are working together to distribute evenly the weight throughout the foot.

For this kind of even distribution to happen, for the foot and ankle to work along horizontal hinges, the outside bone of the lower leg (fibula) and the shin bone (tibia) have to be unglued from one another. Often the web-like structure between them (interosseous membrane) is hard and frozen and limits their ability to help organize the descending weight of the body. By loosening the superficial covering of the leg I give this web a chance to stretch. In later sessions I reach with my fingers directly into this structure.

Even during this first phase of the work I can sometimes get a flat foot to respond or a high rigid foot to begin to relax. The foot begins to become an ever shifting, broadening and recontracting messenger between us and the ground.

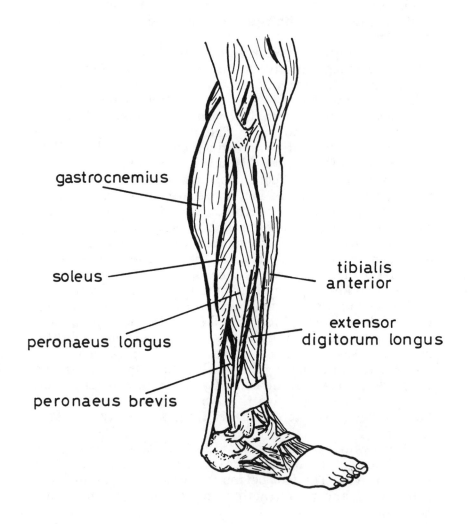

gastrocnemius

soleus

peronaeus longus

peronaeus brevis

tibialis anterior

extensor digitorum longus

PHASE II: ELONGATION

Sensuality and Reaching Out

Consider individuals who have gotten "stuck" during their adolescence. The fear of growing up into responsible adults reveals itself in the way they keep their short, squat, unflexible, half-boyish or girlish forms into adult life. During the second phase, as I work the back of the waist (latissimus dorsi and quadratus lumborum muscle area), I often find an unyielding, fatty accumulation of tissue. I encourage these clients to allow themselves to imagine concurrently with my manipulations of the fascia, what it is for them to be long, supple, and attractive.

On the other hand, there are those individuals with long torsos who are also afraid of their flexibility, their sensuality. If they let go completely they are afraid that they would move too much and would be calling too much attention to themselves, making themselves vulnerable to others. In these cases the waist is long enough, but there is often a protective hardness in the broad back muscles (latissimus dorsi), as well as along the large muscles on each side of the spine (sacrospinalis), a tension that is an attempt to prevent too much movement.

Explore the following fantasy:

Image you are in the center of a large group of people, that you are a beautiful or handsome dancer, perhaps a belly dancer or flamenco dancer. Lift your arms high, exposing your torso, and while twisting and turning, make graceful slow-motion movements. Have the crowd applaud, even whistle and stamp their feet. Let yourself enjoy their admiration.

This second phase involves work at an intermediate depth. I now work with the individual envelopes around large extrinsic muscles, which I consider to be also involved in the armor of the shell. My fingers, knuckles, or elbows now carefully go beyond the superficial layer and begin opening the compartments which surround each muscle. Now I begin to pull apart thickened tissue, which, over a lifetime, has shortened the space in which a muscle can contract and relax and has confused the muscle's movement by gluing it to adjacent compartments with adhesions.

I aim for an elongation of the space between the pelvis and rib cage and an expansion and curving of the sides of the body -- all in preparation for the next phase of more direct work around the pelvis. I encourage lengthening and flexibility so that the individual can begin to vibrate and undulate in wave-like movements through the hips, belly, diaphragm, back, and chest. When a person allows themselves to be long, free, and exposed, these streaming movements originate from inside as well as outside. Lengthening and increasing the mobility of the waist helps prepare the way for the next task, freeing and repositioning the pelvis.

Length and mobility also give a new shape to the torso. In the short, squat figure there is a rounding-out or ballooning of the guts and waist, in which the ribs can no longer function as guides for the tissue. The tissue spills over the rib cage and the ribs themselves bear too much weight, the eleventh and twelveth ribs dipping down into an overarched back, or the upper ribs of the chest collapsing with the weight of unfulfilled emotion.

On the other hand, in the case of a tight-bellied, muscular figure there is a squaring, a flattening-out of the front and back, such that there are no sides to the body, no connecting shapes. Our consciousness is also square. We are aware of ourselves in front or in back, but there is little relation between the two. Release of the torso gives us a more oval shape, a shape which efficiently connects every part of us -- front, back, and sides. The oval shape also allows our energy to radiate out from the core.

Let's look at another important function of the torso. The flexibility of the torso has much to do with the way we use our arms. When we hold ourselves back, we express a double message: our arms are rotated open, expressing our desire for contact (teres minor and infraspinatus) but

Explore the large wing-like muscles along the side of your torso (latissimus dorsi). When our arms are turned inward (medially rotated) in over-protection or over-readiness, the tension of the latissimus is evident all along the back, and forward under the arms. You can see in weightlifters, who have developed enormous and inappropriate wings for themselves, how the shoulder blades and shoulders are also awkwardly pulled forward.

You can work with a part of this structure yourself. After having prepared your energy with deep breathing, reach across with your right hand, sliding your fingers under your left latissimus. If you lift your left arm and press your right hand far enough you can even slide under the shoulder blade. Slowly increasing your pressure, rotate your lifted arm inward (medial) until you feel your hand interacting with these muscles under the shoulder (the subscapularis is also involved). This is an area where you may feel very vulnerable. Allow yourself to be fully conscious of and to express any fears which you may have tucked under your arm.

Relax and see if your arm will now naturally rotate more toward the outside (laterally). After having accepted some of your hidden fears, do you feel more open and receptive?

are pulled back (triceps and deltoids), showing our reluctance and fear. In contrast we may let the arms go forward in readiness or neediness (biceps and deltoids) but collapse the chest. In another variation we rotate our arms inward (medial) and almost cover our genitals, shortening the trunk and closing ourselves by wrapping our wings (latissimus dorsi) around our sides.

Our bodies show how we get trapped in holding ourselves back or in collapsing into unsatisfied neediness. When the torso opens along the sides, and under and around the arms, shoulders, and upper chest, we begin to release these blocked feelings and to find a more balanced way to reach out to the world, a way of talking and holding without losing our centers.

Try an exercise which is sometimes called the "crab."

Lie on your back with your knees bent. With each exhalation let your bent knees flop apart while you reach upward with your arms. Reach as far as you can and try calling out for someone you need. For example, repeat with each exhalation, "Mommy I need you." Express your neediness by reaching so far that your shoulders are pulled up with your arms and your chin juts up and head falls back. After you have charged and discharged your energy with the crab, try reaching out in a quieter way: keep your chin in and shoulders in place and softly ask for what you need.

In order to free the arms for expressing our needs, the work of this phase, then, continues along the sides of the rib cage up to the shoulders and lower neck. And as the arms and torso begin to work together the breath also becomes freer. During spontaneous breathing, described in the next chapter, the whole thoracic cage ripples with pulsations from bottom to top. Most persons have a need to breathe more fully and freely along their sides, allowing the movement of the ribs all the way around from the sternum to the spine and vertically from the eleventh and twelveth ribs up to the first ribs.

Often free and expansive breathing does not continue up under the arms into the axilla. The upper ribs, especially the first and second, are usually tight, immobile rings which press down and lock our energy and feelings deep inside the inferior shoulder and lower throat. I have found that although many people are very conscious of the top of their shoulders and the middle regions of their necks, the areas in the inferior shoulder, base of the throat, and thoracic inlet are usually quite dead and unconscious. Mobilizing these structures can bring new vitality to the lungs and heart, awakening deep seated sadness and joy.

PHASE III: RELEASE OF THE PELVIS

Deep-Seated Passion

The pelvis is the keystone of our structure. In it lies some of our deepest passions: our longing, excitement, frustration, satisfaction, rage. When any of these feelings, deep-seated in the pelvic bowl, are aroused, feelings in other parts of our structure are also affected. If, in fear, we tilt the pelvis forward and hide our genitals, our chest and arms may be thrust out in compensatory longing and neediness. If we hold our buttocks in chronic contraction as a way of controlling our anger, we may also be tightening the whole trunk, and choking on our held-back emotions.

Try the following:

On your hands and knees curl your pelvis up in front toward your chin as you inhale. As you exhale arch your back and throw your head up, barking out your breath with a loud sound. Begin slowly and increase the rhythm until you are rapidly bellowing with sound and feeling. Notice how the movement of your pelvis may have provoked feelings in other parts of your body? Did you feel angry? Helpless? Locate these feelings.

In the pelvis also lies the physical support, the pelvic floor, for the core of the upper body. The position of this floor determines how well the abdominal contents, the

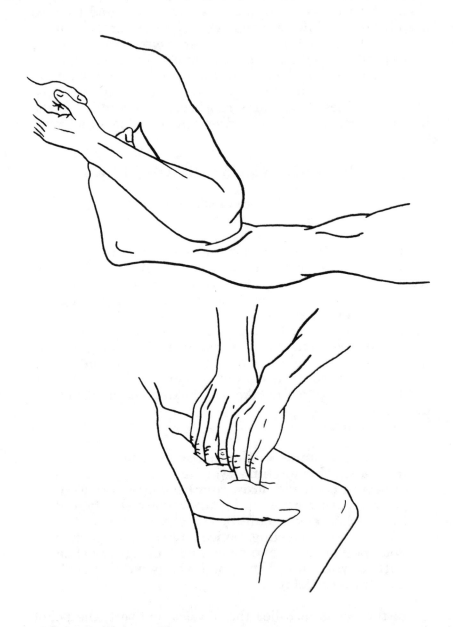

Deep work releases layers of fascia which lie beneath the surface muscles. This work sometimes reaches to the depth where tendons and ligaments attach to the bones.

guts, arrange themselves and how well the shoulders and neck fall into an easy balance on top of the body's core. If we dump the belly over the pelvic brim, not only are the abdominal organs put in stress, but the back and neck have to work hard to keep us from falling forward along with our belly. Or if the buttocks are pulled under -- if we literally tuck our tails -- the belly has to be drawn in and hardened to get our torsos forward again.

This centerpiece of our core connects with the upper and lower body through a complex system of extrinsic and intrinsic muscles -- or more simply outer and inner muscles. There are the large powerful extrinsic muscles which attach partly to the trunk and partly to the limbs. From these we get our prime locomotive power. For example the adductors, which lie on the inside of our thighs, bring our legs together, as when we hold on with our legs during horseback riding. When stuck or overcontracted, they place an inward (medial) pinching pressure on the ischia, our sitting bones. You can see this clearly in women, who as young girls have been taught to keep their legs very close together.

Other examples of extrinsic muscles are the hamstrings and quadriceps, attaching to the front and the back of the pelvis, respectively. These two opposing groups, in addition to their principal function of flexion and extension of the leg, can exert downward force on the posterior or anterior pelvis. In the case of someone with extreme sway back look at how the quadriceps are pulling the pelvis down in front, causing the curve in the back.

Approaching this maze of extrinsic muscle tissue around the pelvis, I gradually work my way into deeper layers of fascia. During the fourth session -- the first of three sessions in this third phase -- I weave my fingers deep under and around the layers of muscles on the inside of the thighs where we hold so much pleasure, rage and fear. By loosening these fascial envelopes we are giving space for the pubis and sitting bones (ischia) at the bottom of the pelvis to move more freely, to become unglued from years of being frozen or pinched in one position,

In session five I reach deeper into the pelvis and other parts of the trunk where we find intrinsic muscles of the core (such as the psoas and pubococcygeous) which help

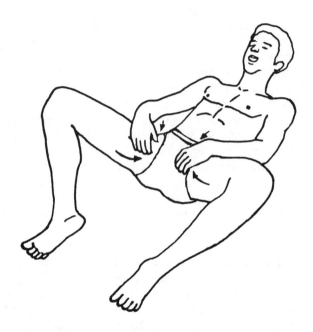

Look in the mirror at the inside of your thighs. Are your legs very close together? Are there curving lines of contracting tension on the inside of your legs? Now lie on your back with your legs spread apart. Breath deeply for five minutes, rocking your pelvis back and forth with each breath, as a warm-up.

With your thumbs and forefingers reach around the large tendons on the inside of your legs just where they reach your genitals. Massage around these tendons while you continue with deep and rather rapid breathing. With your voice and breath express any excitement, anger, or fear which begins to come up inside you. After you are quiet, look in the mirror again. Are the inside of your legs further apart? Do you feel rounder, more open around the inner thigh?

maintain over-all stability and give an initial, subtle impetus to our extrinsic movements. (The psoas is technically extrinsic, since it attaches to the spine and leg, but for all practical purposes it functions like an intrinsic muscle). These intrinsic muscles are often weak and stuck to surrounding structures.

The psoas, lying deep in the pelvic bowl, initiates and guides flexion of the leg at the hip and helps rock the pelvis around its axis, as well. In discussing how the psoas can be overwhelmed by extrinsic muscles, Ida Rolf wrote:

Sadly enough, the psoas is too often unable to play a suitable part in the random individual. It tends to be structurally retired, glued to the pelvic brim. It does not participate in the gait of the average person. Athletic training emphasizes repetitious movement of outer muscles at the expense of the inner (intrinsic); the psoas, more central to the body than the rectus abdominus, succumbs more rapidly to inapproapriate exercise.(2)

The function of the psoas illustrates how we are working to create breadth, length and horizontality in the structure. As the tissue on the sacrum lengthens and broadens, the axis of the pelvis becomes horizontal. The psoas then initiates and guides a smooth, straight, hinge-like movement around this horizontal axis. In a balanced bodymind this hinge will cooperate with the mid-thoracic hinge mentioned above and, as we shall see later, with the cervical hinge at the head.

When working with an individual during this phase of the work, I actively encourage a balancing of the outer and inner muscles (extrinsics and intrinsics). However, I want to help create not just a physical balance, but a bodymind balance as well. For example, when working with the envelopes around the adductors (which pull the legs together and are located on the inner thigh), I often direct clients not only to rock (flex and extend) the pelvis from inside (psoas) but also to allow themselves to become excited, to breathe rapidly, to express their inner and outer sexuality.

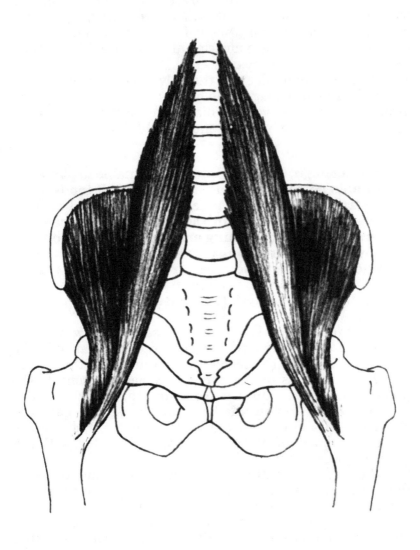

The ilio-psoas, lying deep within the pelvis, functions as an intrinsic muscle. As long as it is not overpowered by extrinsic muscles around the outside of the pelvis, it is a powerful source and regulator of inner energy.

I am grateful to my friend, Margo, a beautiful tantric mistress and author of **Le chemin de l'extase** (3), for helping me accept the sexuality which can arise in working with the pelvis. In the following example Margo and I worked together:

Christina lives in a Stockholm community where sexual freedom is accepted and even expected. Working with the muscle attachments around her anterior and medial thighs, we found them and the surrounding myofascial wrappings, long, thin, glued together, and overcontracted. She kept nervously moving her legs and bouncing her torso without, however, allowing any rotation around the coronal axis of her pelvis. After helping her establish a pattern of deep breathing, we asked her to remain still in her legs and upper torso and to just let her pelvis rock back and forth. As we pressed deeper into the tissue she began to vibrate in gentle rippling waves; and shared with us a feeling of warmth coming from the inner floor of her pelvis. In her sexual life she had been very active, but with rough, explosive, and unsatisfying outer movements which she felt were expected of her. Now her thighs relaxed and looked larger and fuller.

When engaging the extrinsic musculature, it is important to direct attention at the same time to inner activity, feeling, and thought. On the other hand, when working directly with intrinsic structures, clients need to understand and feel how subtle, inner energy can translate evenly into outer movements and attitudes. During direct work on the psoas, I have them shift the whole body toward and into my hands, while encouraging them to let their inner sensations and feelings surface into extrinsic leg and torso movements.

Also when working with the anterior attachments of the pubococcygeous, the main muscle of the pelvic floor, I ask them to take the position given above as an exercise -- on all fours rocking the pelvis back and forth in time with their breathing -- while I press into those parts of the

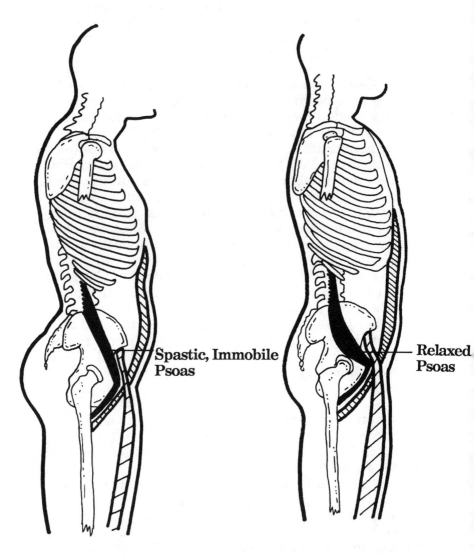

Spastic, Immobile Psoas

Relaxed Psoas

When the belly and thigh muscles (abdominus rectus and rectus femoris) are overdeveloped, they shorten the front of the body, tilting the pelvis forward. The psoas is then frozen in overcontraction. When the thigh and belly soften and lengthen, the pelvis can fall into a balanced position in which the psoas is relaxed but ready to work.

muscles available on either side of the coccyx, as well as the sacrococcygeal ligament. This allows the sacrum to widen and gives the lower back (lumbar spine) a chance to come out of its sway position and begin to shift back (posterior) and get straighter.

Sometimes while I am working in and around the anus, the release of tension explodes into angry pumping and gyrating of the whole pelvis. This is normally followed by a complete relaxation in which the client is thereafter able to accept the authority figures against whom he or she has been holding back energy and anger. Since the anus has often tightened during the anal stage of our infantile development, its release may also affect armor we have developed in the oral or genital phases of our developement. When the anus relaxes often the mouth will also let go and we come into closer contact with our oral needs. Also if the ass has been tucked under with the genitals thrust forward, opening it out may take some of the excessive forward charge off the genitals.

Work on the pelvis is so powerful that we have developed a special process, separate from Postural Integration, which is called Pelvic Sexual Release. In this process we work not only on the outside of the pelvis, but also around and inside the anus and genitals, simultaneously liberating feelings against authority and the desire for genital play and pleasure.

One reason the work around the anus may be so powerful is that in freeing the coccyx and sacrum we are affecting a nerve plexus, the ganglion of impar. This plexus, located between the back wall of the rectum and the coccyx, is a delicate electrical junction of the autonomic nervous system. It appears to have a role in regulating some functions of the circulatory system. Its efficient funtion may help control blood pressure and prevent tachycardia and spastic reactions in the heart. It also appears to function as a kind of connection between the autonomic and central nervous systems.

The work with the anus is generally a part of the overall work of the sixth session, which is along the back of the body and goes deep into the buttocks. Sessions four and five open and lengthen the inside and front of the body. Then, tension shifts to the agonistic groups of muscles on

the back, the area for session six. Reorganizing the back of the body is important not only for releasing the anus and floor of the pelvis (pubococcygeus) as mentioned above, but also for helping unglue the outward rotators of the leg.

Many of us have a tendency to walk slew-footed, pointing one or both of our feet out, like Charlie Chaplin or a circus clown. This may seem comfortable, but the accompanying disorganization of rotators in the back of the pelvis -- piriformis, obturators, gemelli, and quadratus femoris -- leads to confusion up and down the whole length of the back of the body from the heels to the back of the neck. One of the jobs of the sixth session is to release these rotators so that the legs can function straight ahead and the back can lengthen and broaden. Instead of waddling from side to side, we then flow forward on two relaxed parallel lines.

The following exercise can help you get more in touch with the rotators.

While standing, place the feet straight ahead -- not too close together or too far apart, along two parallel lines running through the middle of the ankles, knees, hips, and nipples. Keep your chin tucked in and run in place, leaning the back and the weight of your body forward slightly, but letting the pelvis drop back as if you were dragging a monkey tail on the ground. Be sure that you do not keep your pelvis flat by squeezing your buttocks. Advance but keep your knees fairly high and your stride short. You may look like an Indian on the warpath. Allow your pelvis (and sacrum) to remain flat in the back and feel the psoas muscle initiate the movement of your thighs and feel how light and free your knees and ankles can flow when working on these two parallel lines.

With the release of the rotators there is also a softening and broadening of the sacrum and lower back. The sacral tissue is no longer stuck to the bone and glides easily downward in synchronization with diaphragmatic breathing. But the complete release of the sacrum also depends on a lengthening of the backs of the legs. Crucial

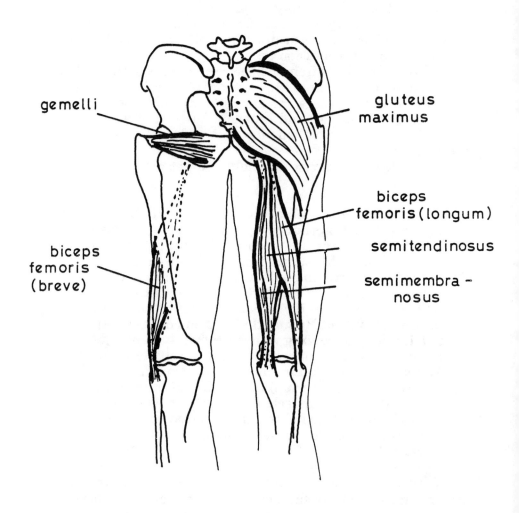

gemelli

gluteus
maximus

biceps
femoris(longum)

semitendinosus

semimembra-
nosus

biceps
femoris
(breve)

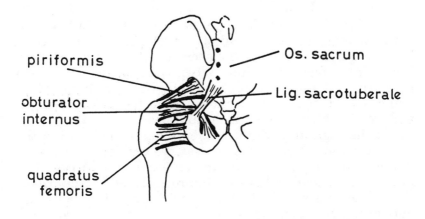

piriformis

obturator
internus

quadratus
femoris

Os. sacrum

Lig. sacrotuberale

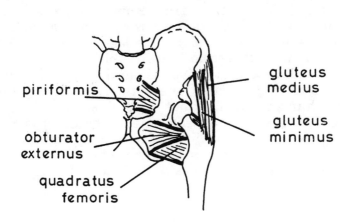

piriformis

obturator
externus

quadratus
femoris

gluteus
medius

gluteus
minimus

to this lengthening is the freeing of the Achilles' tendon and repositioning of the heel bone (calcaneus).

The heel bone is usually held too high by a chronic overcontraction of the Achilles' tendon. The elevated heels we wear and our tendency to walk by lifting the thigh, rather than using our ankles, contribute to this shortening and also shove the heel forward toward the ball of the foot (metatarsal hinge). By creating more distance between the front of the foot and the heel and by stretching out the Achilles' tendon, we encourage the heel to distribute evenly more (though not too much) of our weight. We may come back on our heels more. The sacrum will then move into a flatter and freer position. When this happens we are accepting our unique evolutionary heritage of having and using a calcaneus which allows us to be easily upright and free to better use our arms and heads.

At the beginning of this section I pointed out that in the pelvic release phase of the process, we are dealing with the keystone of body alignment and character structure. Two fictional characters illustrate the role played by the pelvis. Donald Duck is squat. His legs and feet are rotated laterally outward. His pelvis is tilted, dumping his belly forward. He is a classic anal type: stuck, frustrated, angry, and mocked by continual defiance of his attempts to exercise authority. He never learns from his experiences. Pinocchio, the second character, has a pelvis that supports his rib cage and head. It allows his legs to function freely underneath him. Pinocchio is at first phallic. Although he is young and somewhat naive, he survives his difficulties and keeps moving forward. He eventually becomes genital, that is, human. He fills out with flesh and becomes mature. This is a story of pelvic orientation but it is also a story of how the inner qualities of receptivity and openness lead toward extrinsic strength, whereas extrinsic toughness without inner sensitivity leaves one hopelessly stranded.

Donald Duck and Pinocchio show us how the orientation of the pelvis determines character. Donald, with tilted pelvis, arched back and splayed feet, is angry and stuck. Pinocchio, whose pelvis supports and organizes his whole structure, is open to change.

PHASE IV: RELEASE OF HEAD AND NECK

Getting Out of the Head

The fourth phase in the process of release brings us to the head and neck. This area of the body is made up of a maze of small interior muscles and myofascial sheaths, surrounded by outer protective layers. Inside the mouth, throat, nose, and eyes are tissues which hold deep and intense emotions, and which in evolutionary terms can be seen as part of our primitive mammalian and earlier reptilian beginnings.

We hold back these basic emotions and attitudes in our neck or heads by reacting to the traumas and difficulties of life which we do not want to face. The adolescent, not being able to satisfy his or her sexual longings may turn to intellectual pursuits. The young baby which cannot fully support its own head, having experienced the shock of its head accidently falling from a pillow or off a shoulder, begins to stiffen its neck into a chronic attitude of anticipation and distrust.

Deep work on the intrinsic structure of the head plays two special roles. It gives an outlet for the expression of intrinsic feelings locked lower, in the pelvic core, and it helps connect the whole intrinsic structure of the person from the pelvis, upward through the heart, all the way to the head.

If the traditional Rolfing sequence were followed exactly, the pelvis would be worked on before the inside of the head is released. This approach is in contrast to the strategies developed by Reich.(4) Reichians focus their attention on the armor of the eyes, mouth, and throat before moving downward along the body toward the intrinsic armor inside the pelvis. They consider it important to mobilize and open the energy of the head so that the potentially explosive feelings released by work on the pelvis can be channeled out of the person through the head, that is, by screaming, crying, biting, sucking, etc.

For this reason, even during the initial phase of work with the superficial fascia, I begin to work with the head

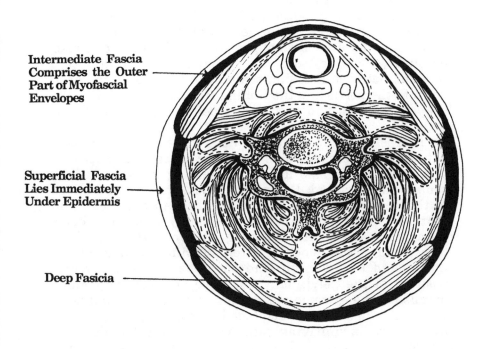

Intermediate Fascia Comprises the Outer Part of Myofascial Envelopes

Superficial Fascia Lies Immediately Under Epidermis

Deep Fasicia

This cross-section of the neck shows an outer superficial layer, an intermediate layer, and deep layer of fascia. The deep fascia is a complicated maze of myofascial sheaths (dashed lines), holding deep and intense emotions. Since the head and neck are an outlet for energy released in other parts of the body, it is important that the practitioner work frequently with these deep, intrinsic structures in the neck.

(inside the mouth and nose, for example). By the time I reach the third phase, release of the pelvis, the head is already sufficiently free to provide a channel for venting the deep frustration and anger that is usually locked in the pelvis.

Experience has shown me, however, that there is a danger in working too much too soon on the emotionallly primitive structures of the head. Some prior work on the pelvis may be a necessary preparation for the head also, because we can be too much "in our heads." Therefore, I combine both the Reichian strategy of going from the head down to the pelvis and the Rolfing strategy of beginning the deepest work in and around the pelvis, then going to the head.

Releasing the inside of the head and neck is important not just as an escape valve for pelvic energy and release of our armor. It is also a way of creating a more unified, connected bodymind. During the work, the sexual feelings in the pelvis can join a loving openness in the chest, and continue upward to the expressive energy of the head itself. So again I stress that focusing on one part of the body (bodymind) is not enough. After softening the pelvic area, inside and out, I often find that the actual structural position of the pelvis may not have changed very much because of the extreme misalignment of the neck and head. When the head is so displaced (for example, as in an overeager, hard-driving man who is literally ahead of himself), extensive work around the pelvis (in an attempt to ease a severely arched back), has little visible effect until the neck and head are able to move back toward the vertical line of body balance.

The tissue which pulls the neck forward is a hardened maze of facial sheaths (thyroid, carotid, and deep cervical) which is anchored on one end by the tongue and on the other by the middle of the back of the neck (mid-cervical vertebrae). To release this we work directly on the base of the tongue, along the soft gums under the tongue, where lots of very early memories are stored. After this work the mouth is not only roomy, the back of the neck softens, fills out, and shifts back as well.

We are again working with horizontality. The tissue which wraps around the neck, in pulling the neck

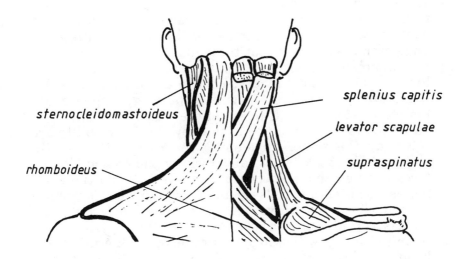

sternocleidomastoideus

splenius capitis

levator scapulae

suespinatus

rhomboideus

forward, functions somewhat like a malfunctioning psoas. When we expand and lengthen the neck, we give this tissue a chance to settle backward, just as the psoas can also shift, and to work much less. The chin can then drop forward easily and there is space for the uppermost vertebrae (atlas and axis) to bend. Working with the base of the occiput (ligamentum nuchae) gives these vertebrae an encouraging tilt forward. This freed hinge at the neck and head now begins to work with the lumbo-dorsal hinge at the pelvis which we previously discussed.

Besides the neck, another important part of horizontality is the movement of the skull. If the neck and chin are forward (or in rare cases too far posterior) the connections of the skull (the fontanelles) will mirror this stress. When the chin is forward the head may come to a point in front (at the anterior fontanelle) and flatten in the back. It is difficult for many people even scientists, to understand and accept that these junctions of our skull are not immobile, fused bone, that parts of the skull can literally move and breathe.When a released head rides horizontally, the skull is subtly pulsing -- in a more limited version of what we see in the throbbing fountain of an infant's forehead. Some of the keys to this mobility are releasing the scalp, broadening the roof of the mouth, shifting the cheek bones, and rocking the sphenoid bone (goes through the head behind the eyes). When the skull moves, the breath travels up and down the whole structure in fine vibrations. Have you ever noticed how light the statues of Mercury appear? He is flying (vibrating, communicating) with wings that come out of the side of his head, at the tiny junction of several skull bones (the pyterion fontanelle).

When the neck and head are released, several of the unconscious regulatory centers (autonomic ganglia) of our nervous system are also released. The superior autonomic cervical ganglion which controls the eyes, ears, and inside of the head; the middle ganglion which controls the heart and circulation; the lower ganglion which controls the heart, lungs, and respiration; and the Vagus nerve -- all begin to have more freedom not only to do their own work better but to cooperate with each other. Here the work on different parts of the structure really begins to create

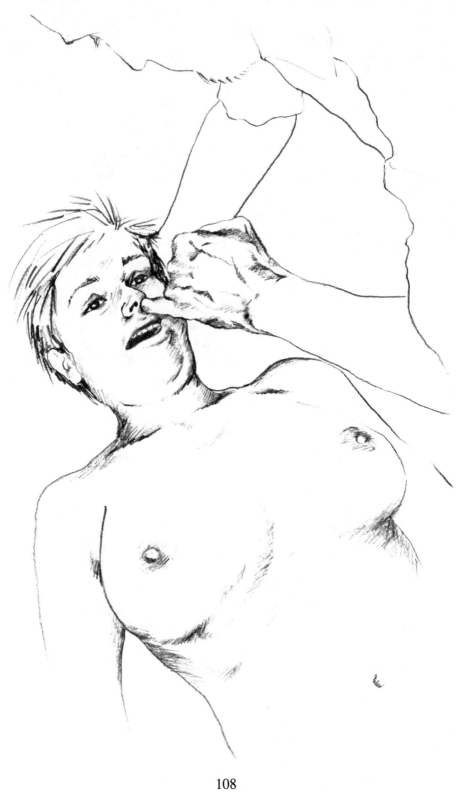

reciprocal effects. Work with the ganglion of impar, during the sixth session, now leads to a subtle electrical harmony up and down the centers (plexi) of the autonomic system. This kind of interaction helps to retune the nervous system. In the next section I want to outline a theory of nervous response, the gate theory, which partially explains how this retuning can take place during wholistic bodywork.

Creating alignment between the pelvis and head involves the rib cage, which needs to open radially like a parachute or umbrella, allowing the head to rock on top and the pelvis and legs to seemingly dangle beneath.(5)(See the illustration near the beginning of Chapter V). That is, of course, a general change, a whole bodymind phenomenon. The hard-driving man settles back into his center only as he lets go of his heady ambitions and repressed sexual energy. He can then become receptive in his heart to his real needs.

To feel the connection between the neck, back, and pelvis try the following exercise:

> **Sit on the edge of a chair with your feet on the floor. Let your arms rest at your sides, but keep your shoulders in place. Begin at the uppermost vertebrae (atlas and axis) and drop your neck (and only your neck), one vertebra at a time. When you have reached the bottom of the neck, then continue, one vertebra at a time, down the spine until you reach the coccyx. Return to a upright position, stacking one vertebra on top another, one at a time. Be sure not to use your head to lift yourself back into position. After several of these spinal rolls notice the continuity of your neck, back and pelvis, and how they flow in coordination with each other.**

At this stage of the process (work on the head) the overall release has reached a point where our concern goes beyond merely freeing the old armor locked in individual body segments. Now we are beginning to pay attention to the need for these segments to move together in balance with one another. This is the goal of the second stage, sessions 8, 9, and 10 -- the integration of bodymind -- which

If you thrust your neck forward and lift your chin too high, part of the problem is at the back of the neck where the long muscles on either side of the vertebrae are pulling down on the back of the skull. Since the head works on a horizontal axis, it needs to tilt forward and down, while the muscles at the nape of the neck relax and lengthen.

Place your elbows on a table as if to prop up your head, but place your fingers at the back of your head. While breathing deeply, let your chin drop, flatten the back of your neck and push your head down between your hands, sliding your fingers into the tissue at the base of the head. Let your fingers go deep into and across the two rope-like structures (capitus muscles). Be sure not to lift your chin. Imagine your neck and back elongating like a fishing pole slightly bent over the water.

To be long and tall you do not need to lift your chin. Length comes from a relaxation of the spine, not from the overeagerness and excessive trying of holding ourselves high with our chins and noses.

is covered in the next chapter. Before going into the process of integration, let us look further at the process of release, now from the point of view of the client's experience.

THE EXPERIENCE OF RELEASE

Contacting, Acknowledging, and Claiming Ourselves

The stage of release helps the individual dissolve the protective armor which has accumulated in the various segments and layers of bodymind. Release is gradually felt and noticed as the tissue softens, movements become freer, and thoughts and feelings are liberated. This process is far from being merely a technical or mechanical change. As we shall see in Chapter VI, practitioners are responsible for being sensitive to how much pressure individuals can tolerate at a given moment. They need to work on the border between relaxing massage and a deeper and sometimes painful penetration of the muscle tissue. If the pressure is too light, nothing new is evoked; if too deep or rapid, then the armor simply reinforces itself. Individuals need to be confronted by their armor, but at a rate which gradually allows time to assimilate and explore what is happening. Finally, however, it is up to the individual to be receptive to the work of the practitioner, to experience those parts of the self which have been previously rejected and made unconscious.

As explained in the previous chapter, whether armor takes the form of a hard defense or soft cushion, it is initially developed as a way of avoiding pain and dissatisfaction, but becomes the habitual means by which we unconsciously hold on to pain. For us to experience this armor is for us to liberate ourselves from past attitudes and postures, but this in no sense is an avoidance or destruction of our unique personal histories. Encountering our armor is a distinct process in which we are freed from the past, and yet at the same time, make it a part of us. In

111

order to be free from our armor we not only have to contact it and acknowledge its role in our lives, we also have to claim it as a part of us.

Often we so deaden ourselves that we become totally unconscious of our defenses and continually create an environment where we need not encounter any problems. Everything is carefully made safe and uneventful. The first condition for transformation is to sense and feel our incompleteness, to be frustrated. During the release stage of Postural Integration, there comes a point at which clients begin to experience their resistance to change. Without this first step, no amount of tissue manipulation, deep breathing, guided movement, or spiritual and mental affirmation can bring about a significant and lasting release of bodymind armor.

The second step in the experience of release is the acknowledgment or recognition that frustration, this sense of incompleteness, is the problem itself. So long as daddy, mommy, or society serve as the scapegoat of causing my problem, I will remain stuck, even if I am aware that I have a problem. Equally, if it is "that backache," or "those aching feet," which controls me, I have not yet acknowledged or recognized my armor for what it is, namely my defense against myself. The release I feel in letting go of my armor is not a mysterious event in which my burdens are relieved by some outside force. As the practitioner impinges on my body, I need to be willing to say "I'm resisting." With this recognition I may be feeling my struggle with myself, or I may simply be noting my resistance.

Finally as a last step in the process of letting go of my armor, I need to claim my incompleteness, my pain and dissatisfaction as an important and welcome part of me. Now that I am responsible for creating my pain, I also accept it as a vital and valuable part of me. Here there is a seeming paradox: the moment I really accept my unwanted attitude, I become free from it. For example, when I accept my hatred for my father, the hate becomes complete, whole, and powerful, and I am ready for other feelings. Now that I hate my father I can also more fully love him. The pain that emerges from deep tissue work is transformed. It is no longer raw pain but an accepted and claimed part of me which is no longer simply pain, but rather a release from an old hurt. I become free from my past by making it a part of me.

In order to better understand how old pain is transformed into a new free experience, we need a view of human consciousness which does not treat our bodies as objects to be analyzed and manipulated. In many of the classical western models of consciousness, consciousness is located in one place, "here," while the object is located "there," and we try to extend our awareness under controlled conditions by analyzing different parts of the object or event. According to this view, I see the pain in my lower back as a problem to be studied, as the effect of causes which I hope can eventually be understood and eliminated. But this separation of the pain from me is the problem. As noted earlier, so long as I deal with my pain as something foreign to me, I armor myself against the possibility of truly exploring the pain and being released from it.

Both the Zen and Gestalt views of consciousness make clear how the experience of being released is a process of claiming previously foreign parts of ourselves. When I fully contact, acknowledge, and claim a part of myself I am no longer just conscious of it as a separate object, I become the object. In Zen I totally blend with the object; I am both the observer and observed. Experiment with the following.

At the toy store buy a bow and arrow set which has snubnosed rubber arrows which stick to the point of impact. Set up a target only a few yard away. Try hitting the target a few times. Next, while blindfollowed meditate on the target and feel yourself merging with it. Now shoot again, but this time sense that you are shooting a part of yourself. After improving at a short distance increase the range. This is an exercise which needs to be practiced frequently and clearly depends also on your developing capacity to meditate.

In Gestalt therapy, I illuminate the partly unconscious background of my experience by letting the unconscious part of me speak out. As the practitioner encountered the well-developed armor of my lower back, I felt the contact, I acknowledged my resistance to what lies deep inside me, and now finally I begin to claim my lower back by being there in it, talking from there to myself. "Jack, I'm hurting; you've got to slow down the everyday pace and give me the attention I deserve." Even if this dialogue goes no further, I have already begun to release the unconscious defense which I have stored in my back. But as we shall see in the next chapter, this dialogue can continue. Not only can I release my armored parts, I can, through the released parts, now communicate with other aspects of myself which need to cooperate with each other, which need to try out new movements, feelings, and thoughts.

Another way of understanding the experience of being released from our past postures and attitudes is to look at the pain which emerges as a special, transforming event in the nervous system. According to one of the most commonly accepted explanations of the nature of pain, the specificity theory (6), a simple outside stimulus to the nerve endings in the muscle tissue leads to a general conditioned response experienced as pain, but this does not account for the direct contribution of local tissue (and its muscle memory) to the experience of pain. What is experienced as pain depends not just on the response in the brain (and in turn on subsequent generalized responses in the whole system) but also on how the local tissue allows the stimulus to be received into the system. The specificity theory does not adequately account for the role which armor and the release of armor play in determining the reaction to the stimulus.

An alternative way to look at pain is to see the nervous system as a reciprocal unit with changes in any one part affecting every other part. Overall nervous activity is then not solely controlled by the brain stem, but lower centers also play a critical role. According to this view, as we saw earlier, the nervous system is taken as a complicated set of gates which open and close as stimuli pass through local receptors. What I feel locally depends not merely on the response in the brain alone, but in addition on how local tissue controls these gates. It is as if the gates in a certain part of bodymind were "set" by a previously painful

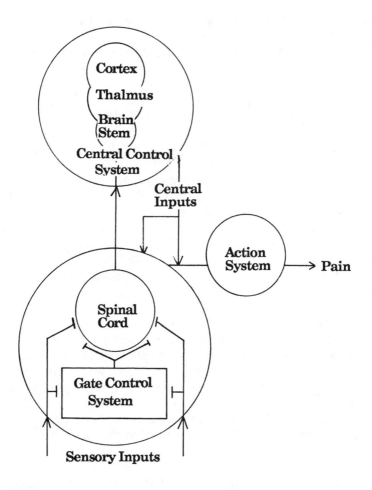

According to one of the classical explanations, pain is a *conditioned response in the brain to a simple outside stimulus to the tissue. But this view does not account for the contribution which local tissue makes to the experience of pain. What we experience as pain depends on how local tissue allows the stimulus to be received; it depends on the "memory" held in the tissues. Here we see an alternative to the classical model. The nervous system is a reciprocal unit, such that changes in any one part affect every other part. The nervous system uses a complicated set of gates which open and close as stimuli pass through local receptors.*

experience, set by a protective armor which "freezes" the tissue in and around the muscle.

If armor were to be considered permanent and unchangeable, the specificity theory of simple stimulus and response could account for much of our "stuck" behavior, for the gates would remain in their habitual positions and their influence would always be the same. However, during the process of releasing our armor, through deep bodywork, it seems that we may "reopen" some of the gates previously set by our experience. In this view when the practitioner penetrates the body defenses, the tissue is restimulated and the client may re-experience the memories, the events held in the muscles. It seems that the act of fully re-experiencing pain is a part of the process of dissolving armor. Thereafter the gates are no longer set by our armor, but are free, as we shall see in a later chapter, to be reset for new kinds of integrating experiences.

Hilda came with a chronic neck problem. As I worked in the fascia of her neck during the seventh session, she at first tensed her shoulders, neck, and head, and groaned in resistance to even my very slow entry between the large lateral muscles. I asked her to put her awareness into these muscles and to actually "become" her neck. She first spoke defensively, "We're afraid you're going to hurt us even more." Then, "We're such hard muscles; we are tired of being on guard all the time." I encouraged her to let herself feel more pain. Suddenly a long forgotten event came back in vivid detail. "I'm running through the backyard, hitting the clothesline. I'm going unconscious." She felt she was dying. I told her to go ahead and let herself experience the death, which she had hidden in her neck all these years. Hot flashes and vibrations ran up and down her whole body. An immense joy welled up inside her and her neck softened and lengthened. She now wanted to turn and swing her head for the first time since she could remember.

FOOTNOTES FOR CHAPTER III

1. See A. Forster, **Ueber die morphologische Bedeutung des Wangenfettpfropfes**; A. Richet, **Traite pratique d'anatomie medico-chirurgicale**; E. Singer, **Fasciae of the Human Body and Their Relations to the Organs They Develop**; and B.B. Gallaudet, **The Planes of Fascia.**
2. **Rolfing**, p.118.
3. **Le chemin de l'extase**, Mitsou Naslednikov (Paris: Albin Michele, 1981).
4. **Orgone, Reich, And Eros**, op.cit.
5. Compare with images in:
   The Thinking Body, Mary E. Todd (New York: Dance Horizons, 1973).
6. **The Puzzle of Pain**, p.126.

CHAPTER IV
BALANCE, BREATH, AND ENERGY

Deliberately try to place yourself in a more upright position. Notice that if you are trying to hold your shoulders back, you must tighten the muscles between your shoulder blades, and at the same time, while lifting your chest, you probably must arch your back. If you habitually hold your shoulders back and also keep your pelvis straight, notice how chronically tense your belly and buttocks have become. Whenever we try to find a better physical balance by intentionally holding ourselves in what we consider a good posture, we either only temporarily succeed in rearranging isolated parts of our structure, or if we do manage to maintain a more erect position for any length of time, we make ourselves rigid and inflexible.

Now try to totally relax. You may find that you feel comfortable in completely passive positions, e.g., lying down, but if you try to sit, stand, or walk in a relaxed way, you will probably find yourself collapsing and slouching more than ever. This demonstrates that we can relax and stretch our muscles only to the extent that the surrounding thickened, myofascial structures permit.

Sometimes we may alternate between trying to hold ourselves upright and letting go of our tensions. But our discomfort in either case usually increases with age, and our overall flexibility decreases as our tissues become thicker and more restricted.

From an emotional and mental point of view we may find ourselves trapped in an endless cycle of elation and depression. Consider Edith Piaf, who between birth and death rose from street singer to celebrated chanteuse, in a roller-coaster life of stardom and failure, comeback and collapse, love and death. When the prospect of living such a life of ups and downs feels too risky or exhausting, we may settle for an even, safe, half-conscious existence somewhere in between.

The alternative to these traps we create in our bodies and minds is a unified bodymind balance which is flowing, and while encompassing a wide range of experience, is still stable. The first step toward such a balance is to release the tension we have accumulated in restricted muscles and in blocked feelings and thoughts. When we begin opening ourselves, begin letting go both inside and out, we dissolve our old, protective armor and become more spontaneous.

The second step is to establish an integrating pattern within ourselves by which we can move from one posture and experience to another, without losing our sense of continuity. This is the task of the second stage of wholistic bodymind work, sessions 8, 9, 10. In explaining this stage we need first to look at what constitutes balance, and how breathing is an essential part of balance (as well as the previous release). In the next chapter, "Fine Tuning Bodymind" we can then turn to the details of the integration process.

BALANCE AS CIRCULATING ENERGY
Uninterrupted Flow

In the here and now there is no protective core and shell, only the rhythm of our energy as we flow naturally outward and inward, like the ebb and flow of the tides. This rhythm, seen from a physical perspective, is a free movement of the whole body as a single, functional, and integrated unit. It is a rocking and vibrating which is part of a vertical wave, travelling back and forth between the feet and head. From an emotional perspective feelings melt into one another. The inner and outer release of my anger, for example, may open me to joy and allow me to become more receptive, sadder, or even afraid. From a cognitive perspective my thoughts are insights which are continually being modified by the ever-changing outer demands of my practical experience.

While receiving a session of bodywork from my friends, Blanca Rosa Anorve (director of El Instituto del Postural Integration in Mexico) and Dr. Rafaelle Estrada Villa (psychiatrist and director of El

Instituto Wilhelm Reich), I felt an intense sadness welling up inside me. Unlike the other times when I had to some extent let myself cry, this time I sobbed uncontrollably and to my surprise a fluttering, vibrating sensation spread from inside my chest to every part of my body. And it wasn't just sadness. It was joy, acceptance, love, anger, and fear, all flowing back and forth through each other, yet each retaining its distinctive character. I realized then how I had been using one feeling to cancel out another, and how I could now surrender completely to new feelings without losing old ones.

At every level of bodymind -- the physical, emotional, and mental, as well as the inside and outside -- our sense of unity comes from us permitting one experience to follow another without interference. We have seen that when we try to preserve the past as a protection against what was once painful, we divide and armor ourselves. However, a unified experience of the self is not merely the freedom to change from one moment to the next, it is also a process which has continuity and is self-nourishing. Energy builds and releases, then begins again. Emotions are aroused and expressed, then later provoked again. Thoughts begin, reach conclusions, then reconfirm or modify themselves. This cycle of energy differs from change which loses this continuity. It is an energy different from a roller-coaster life of ups and downs in that each experience of bodymind is complete in itself, yet leads to the next experience without interruption. Body actions complete themselves, as they lead into new patterns. Emotions are fully expressed, yet contribute to new feelings. Thinking becomes a continuum of revisable conclusions. It is the very act of being complete which gives the energy and freedom for the next moment of experience to be a new unarmored beginning. In my work with Blanca Rosa and Rafaelle I realized that I was free to commit myself completely to building and expending my energy in each moment.

We can also look at this cycle in terms of our internal and external experience. We may choose to contract, to withdraw our energy into our inside selves, then release this stored energy outward. The completeness and continuity of this movement lies in this: only if we permit our energy fully to accumulate inwardly can we expend it completely outwardly. This cycle was clear to me as I worked with Blanca and Rafaelle. With each "sob," I felt myself pull in and then explode out. And it was my willingness to allow this to continue that sustained me.

In the previous chapters I refered to this cyclic movement as the charge and discharge of energy. We gradually increase our energy to a maximum harmonious level, then empty ourselves, discharge ourselves, in preparation for the next oncoming experience. This is similar to what Reich called the four beat formula -- tension, charge, discharge, relaxation.(1) I have also found, like Reich, that unhindered breathing is the key to helping us achieve a free flow of our energy, to find a balance between our charging and discharging activities. I want to turn shortly to how free breathing encourages a release of armor and helps us find this kind of circulating balance, but first I want to mention some other ways of seeing balance as the outcome of a cycle of energy.

Take a comfortable position for deep breathing. Begin breathing slowly, then gradually increase your rhythm. Try going faster and slower. Sometimes inhale more than exhaling; sometimes exhaling more than inhaling. After five or ten minutes of experimenting with your breath find a tempo which suits you and continue for fifteen or twenty minutes without interruption. Did you discover that your breathing at a certain point became effortless and that your inhalations and exhalations became equal?

I have been looking at individual moments of experience as that which moves through a cycle of change. But we can also take the whole span of life as cyclic. Each of us is born, matures, dies, and some part of us contributes to ongoing life. Very often we have become blocked at or before birth and simply play out this armored role over and over again throughout our lives. If we labored long to enter the world, we may work hard to complete everyday tasks. If we were lifted out of the womb by caesarian intervention, we may be inclined to let things happen to us. When we are willing to explore our unconscious attitudes toward birth, by a kind of rebirthing, we are learning to surrender and renew every moment of ourselves by accepting and using our past experience. We are creating a self-nurturing, balanced flow in our lives. We shall later see how the experience of rebirth can enhance the process of integration during deep bodywork.

We shall also see how I apply to deep bodywork an ancient Chinese view of balance being cyclic. According to the Taoist model of the five elements, used in acupuncture (or acupressure), there is a deep circulation of "chi," that is, vital energy. It is organized into elements corresponding to the seasons of the year: Water for winter; Wood for spring; Fire for summer; Earth for late summer; and Metal for autumn. When our chi is healthy, it flows unblocked from one element to the next, just as the seasons of the year pass one into another. If, for example, we develop too much fire, too much enthusiasm, we may be overtaxing a part of ourselves, taking away from the next element, earth, which allows us to mellow out and be receptive to circulating chi energy.

Finally there is another way we can look at balance as cyclic. When we are balanced we are also in physiological and gravitational harmony with ourselves and the earth. In the previous chapter we saw how in the release of stuck fascia we give freedom to the muscles to equalize their contractions with each other in order to balance and align the major segments of the body. But this is not a static condition. In upright body balance there is constant movement, a subtle wave of contractions and counter contractions, which passes back and forth between the feet and head. It is when we try to hold on to a given upright position that we begin to armor ourselves and prevent the planes of fasciae from carrying the fine cyclic vibration.

BREATH AND RELEASE
Completely Charging and Discharging

Before considering the essential role of breathing in bodymind balance, let us consider the role of breathing during release, the first stage of the process. With the release of tension in the body tissue, the practitioner is working with the habitual ways in which we block and control our breath. If we take in too much air -- the extreme would be gasping for air -- we build our energy without fully expending what is accumulating. On the other hand, if we throw out our breath with an extended, contracting exhalation, and delay our need for incoming air, we literally overextend ourselves -- we use ourselves up. We may see examples of this every day. There is the aggressive, active male who keeps his chest puffed out, or the passive, listless female who collapses her chest and tightens her diaphragm.

You can experiment with these energies and positions:

Inhale so deeply and high in your chest that your torso is drawn backwards. Do not exhale fully, but inhale again as deeply as possible. Continue this pattern for several minutes. Do you feel like you are holding back your power and feelings?

Now try the opposite. Exhale as completely as possible, but do not inhale fully. Continue for several minutes. Do you feel like you are giving your energy away? That you are collapsing?

One way of releasing armor is to encourage the client to increase the energy disequilibrium even further. When a person is overcharged, I may encourage a still greater charge through deeper, more rapid inhalations, until the energy buildup finally has to surge into a discharge. On the other hand, when a person is undercharged, I may then encourage even more exhalation, until in exhaustion, a greater inhalation automatically occurs and the person recharges. My entry into the body tissue is coordinated with these breathing patterns. Often I use provocative, quick palpations along with strong exhalations to bring energy past the point of release, then I work with very slow maneuvers and slow inhalations, while shifting and organizing layers of fascia.

Juan was a Mexican joker. He laughed uproariously at his own jokes, even to the point of coughing and almost strangling. When I tried to touch him he giggled and wiggled away from me. There was no chance at this stage that I could work slowly with him in any way. I had him exhale as hard and as fast as he could, while I persistently goosed, grabbed, poked, and jabbed his body. His hysterical laughter eventually turned into rage, then exhaustion. Finally, while he inhaled gently and fully, I could slowly hook my fingers across the large fascial wrappings around his chest.

Another way of releasing armor is to take attention away from that part of the breathing cycle which is overworked and focus on the neglected part. If a client's exhalation is excessive, if there is too much discharge, I often help in softening and slowing down the exhalation, while supporting deeper inhalations, especially in those areas of the chest, belly, or back which are neglected. Conversely, when the inhalation is too great, I shift attention from deep breathing to a larger exhalation, often encouraging exaggerated force and sound. In these cases, I move my hands slowly and deeply, while focusing on either inhalation or exhalation.(2)

Look at yourself in the mirror. Examine the relation between your upper chest and diaphragm. Are you more expanded, and do you inhale more above in the chest or below in the diaphragm? If you see that you neglect your diaphragmatic inhalations, take a position on your back, prop your pelvis high on your elbows and breathe into your belly and lower back. Breathe only below, not in the chest. Begin slowly and gradually increase the rhythm of inhalation and exhalation, making sure the inhalation, charge, is greater then the exhalation.

Afterwards do you find your upper and lower inhalation are more equal? Do you feel energized?

If you notice that you neglect inhaling in your chest, lie on your back, and bring your knees over your head, letting them touch the floor or holding them at the farthermost point they will reach. The chin will be tucked into the chest. Pant in short breaths in the upper chest, letting your inhalation be greater than your exhalation. Do not inhale in the diaphragm. Afterwards do you find your inhalation more equalized?

BREATH AND BALANCE

Spontaneous Vibrations

It is not enough, however, to break through and release the breathing blocks and their accompanying armor. There is also a need in our breathing rhythm (and correspondingly in our emotional and mental structures) for a stable pattern of breathing. This balance is not a static, physical place, or an unchanging attitude. It is the dynamic and changing way we maintain the unity of the whole self. The breath functions as a part of the whole bodymind and helps to establish a flexible balance by finding a level of recurring charge and discharge where our energy remains even and self-nourishing.

A complete cycle is not simply a repetitious building of energy followed by a discharge of energy, followed by another recharge. Nor is it an unbroken steady contraction, followed by steady expansion and then another contraction. An unarmored cycle of energy is made up of many smaller cycles, just as a liberating orgasm is a series of lesser, rising and falling orgasms. We see this in the rhythm of a free spontaneous breath.

Whenever I surrender and really let my breathing go, the rhythm is not merely in and out. As I inhale I quiver throughout the rib cage, and my whole breathing apparatus may even momentarily slow or stop the incoming air with subtle counter pressures, then continue with inhala-

126

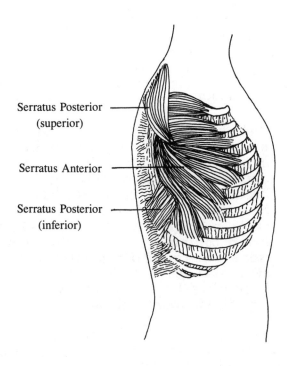

Serratus Posterior
(superior)

Serratus Anterior

Serratus Posterior
(inferior)

The movement of the thoracic cage during spontaneous breathing is an interplay of opposing (agonistic and antagonistic) muscle groups. The superior posterior serratus muscles, in the upper back, and the serratus anterior muscles, extending along the sides of the body, lift and open the rib cage during inhalation. The inferior posterior serratus group, in the lower back, works antagonistically pulling the ribs down and in during exhalation.

tion until I pause again. My inhalation is, then, an accumulation of small inhalations with some small countering exhalation-like movements. My exhalation is just the reverse: exhalations with partial momentary "inhalations."

This action is actually an interplay of the agonistic and antagonistic groups of muscles governing respiration. For example, the superior posterior serratus muscles in the upper back (see the illustration) lift and open the rib cage during inspiration, while the inferior posterior serratus muscles in the lower back pull down and inward during exhalation. In alternating opposed movements, these muscles subtly check and free each other, eventually completely lifting up or pulling down the rib cage.

Take a breath by inhaling in a series of short breaths. Inhale and pause, perhaps even very slightly exhalating, then inhale further and pause, until you are completely filled up. Now let go of your breath by exhaling in a series of short breaths. Make a small, short explosive exhalation, cutting it short, perhaps even allowing a slight inhalation before continuing with another short exhalation. Repeat this cycle of inhalations and exhalations several times. Now breathe normally without hesitating. Do you notice more variability and vibration in your breathing?

Not every inhalation or exhalation moves the total possible volume of air. The volume and depth of the breath varies continually with our physical, emotional, and mental demands, and the breath may change directions at any moment. An inhalation may, part way through, become an exhalation. The overall effect is a rippling, spontaneous rocking of the torso, which spreads up and downward through the whole body.

It is just this spontaneous, variable character of an unarmored breath which permits it to be complete. Each inhalation or exhalation, being free to pause or even reverse itself, is also free, under the right conditions, to fully expand or contract, to be a completely filled or empty breath. When we deliberately try to make breathing

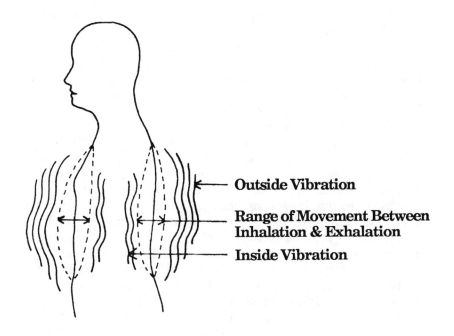

Outside Vibration

Range of Movement Between Inhalation & Exhalation

Inside Vibration

Breathing is a part of our whole bodymind. A spontaneous breath, that is, a breath which is full and free, helps us to establish a flexible center, a place from which our energy, our level of charge and discharge, remains even and self- nourishing. As we inhale, the breath quivers throughout the entire ribcage. We may even momentarily slow or stop incoming air with subtle counter pressure, then continue with inhalation until the next pause. An exhalation may also have these momentary, spontaneous pauses. The overall effect is an inner and outer vibration, which gently rocks the torso, and spreads throughout the body and mind.

"complete," we create tension which prevents the variable streaming of energy necessary to the breath eventually completing its cycle. We then revert to using armored habits, and deal with ourselves as objects, instead of following the rhythm of our changing needs.

The capacity to be flexible in every aspect of bodymind calls for a sustained and equal level of both charge and discharge. The breath now can be charging, or now discharging, but it equalizes itself. In contrast with the initial release stage of work, in which we exaggerate or support over and under-accentuated parts of the breathing cycle, during the integrating stage of Postural Integration, I help clients explore their capacity for variety and duration in breathing. I encourage them to experiment with charging by alternating between rapid and slow, shallow and deep, excited and calm breaths.

Practitioners need to work with such sensitivity to the movement of their clients' breathing that their own bodies and breathing rhythms synchronize with even the slighest change in the direction of the breath. Frequently I take my clients through cycles of charge and discharge where a single charge can be a long series of ever-increasing inhalations, finally reaching a plateau, but the charge does not become excessive because it is always balanced with some discharge. I help them gradually descend from this plateau by focusing on a series of increasing exhalations, until charge and discharge are balanced at a lower level.

One currently popular and effective way to maintain a high, but even, level of balanced charge and discharge is through what Leonard Orr, the creator of a type of rebirthing, calls "the connected breath."(3) This consists of using a series of short, rapid nasal breaths, followed by a slow, surrendering breath. This even, steady charging process helps the us overcome the everyday roles which we use to deaden ourselves -- the role of parent, child, or teacher -- and become connected with our "vertical" spiritual energy.

I have found this style of "connected breathing" to be an important tool in my own bodywork, but for me it seems most effective if it is not a substitution of spiritual energy for the release and integration of the earthly energy we have stored in our bodies, feelings, and thoughts. Rather than overcoming our parent, child, and teacher, we need to

While encouraging full, free breathing, the practitioner connects myofascial planes between different parts of the body.

enter more fully into these roles, accepting and enlarging them with breathing charges and discharges. If we try to transcend them, without completely accepting them, we run the risk of being trapped in the role of a spiritual aspirant.

Here is an example of how connected breathing and rebirthing can enhance bodywork:

> **Kenny felt he had to overcome his dislike for his mother. During releasing work around the pelvis and throat, he had recurring feelings of nausea and had the fantasy that he was flaunting his genitals in front of her. We decided to have the seventh session, which concentrates on the head, in the rebirthing tub (warm Japanese bath) of our institute.**
>
> **I prepared for work inside the mouth by having him float in the warm water in a foetal position, using a snorkel to facilitate breathing. As he started gasping for air and reached a hyper-ventilated state, now above water I work with my fingertips around the base of his tongue and encouraged him not to control his disgust but to affirm it as a natural part of himself. He gagged and convulsed and then suddenly re-experienced the feeling of being suffocated by the over- protective demands of his mother -- in the womb, at birth, during breast feeding.**
>
> **Now his breath became full and quiet, and as we played with soft patterns of charging and discharging, with gentle connected breaths, he saw that on the other side of his disgust there was also a deep love for his mother in which he could say no, yet accept her for what she did and was.**

When breath is used to integrate and give balance, we also begin to connect the parts of our bodies, to allow recurring wave-like movements between feet, legs, pelvis, torso, arms, and head. While encouraging variable and sustained styles of breathing, I use my hands to help my clients find a connection between the fascial sheaths that extend the length of the body. For example, as the breath

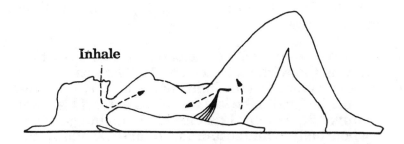

Inhale

Lie relaxed with your back and neck against the floor and with your knees bent. If your back is curved, prop the knees higher with a pillow until the back is flat. If the neck is curved, place a small book under the head. Hold an image of the major extrinsic muscles around the pelvis (belly, buttocks, thighs) being full and soft. Now as you curl the pubic bone toward your chin, using only the intrinsic power of the psoas, inhale while the belly elongates and the chest rises. Uncurl, relaxing the psoas and flattening the back without holding with abdominal muscles.

This position, which can also be done in a standing, monkey-like pose, or while propped against the wall, will help you maintain a good physical balance, even as you move the body from the pelvis. Now, without straining, increase the rate of movement and the breathing rhythm. If you play with this movement and breath, sometimes faster, sometimes slower, sometimes deeper, sometimes more shallow, you can eventually reach a steady, high level of charge and discharge which sustains a fine vibration or streaming throughout the whole body. Notice that in following this energy you may moan, cry, shout, pursue any line of fantasy or thought, without losing any of your awareness, without straining to achieve some prescribed goal.

In this exercise for discovering the psoas I have asked you to inhale as you curl your pelvis upward and to exhale as you uncurl it. Often in bioenergetic exercises the pelvis is moved in just the opposite pattern, with the exhalation accompanying the upward movement of the pelvis. However, the individual is then tempted to use the extrinsic abdominal muscles to lift the pelvis and assist in a complete exhalation. The psoas is overpowered by this action. It can best be gently activated with a charging inhalation, rather than a discharging exhalation. This coordinated breath and movement will not only help your own self-exploration but also will allow the practitioner to press more easily against a relaxed abdominal wall and use his or her hands to reach, and interact directly with the psoas.

begins to flow freely all around the chest and diaphragm and begins to extend itself deeper into the abdomen toward the legs, the layers of fascia between the pelvis and rib cage are ready to stretch and vibrate, creating a rocking and vibrating ripple with each cycle of respiration.

This spontaneous movement of breath and body is, of course, also a movement of feelings and thoughts. They, too, build, change directions, sustain, expend, and renurture themselves:

> **Juan returned for the eighth session. By this time his body had softened and I felt he was ready to begin connecting the high charge he carried in his upper body with the less conscious parts of his lower body. At one point I had him hold an image of his whole body, while sustaining relaxed, shallow, and rapid breathing. I entered slowly and deeply into the rectus muscle on the front of his thigh, while at the same time I pressed my other hand firmly under his diaphragmatic arch.**

> **He felt a hot flash running diagonally across his body between my hands. He shared that his father had made fun of the limp he had had in his leg since childhood and that his laughter was in part a way of blocking out the shame and anger connected with the lower part of his body. I had him relax and as I continued working on both his leg and trunk, he maintained an easy, charging breath and let his feelings toward his father and himself flow in waves the entire length of his body.**

This work with the energy flow in breathing, rebirthing, physical movement, and emotional expression helps establish a delicate, balanced cirulation of energy. At this point, the Chinese techniques of harmonizing the flow of energy through the elements of water, wood, fire, earth, and metal become useful. We saw earlier that an excess in one element can prevent the next element from receiving enough energy. I discovered that Juan allowed his fire element to build to the point where it robbed the next element, earth, that is, receptivity, of its needed energy. While working with his breath and the movement of his body, I pressed points to enhance his earth energy, to convert his excessive exuberance and laughter into a more mellow receptivity.

Now that we have examined the cyclic nature of balance and how one uses breathing to help create it, let us turn to the steps involved in achieving this balance.

FOOTNOTES FOR CHAPTER IV

1. **The Function of the Orgasm**, Wilhelm Reich (New York: Noonday Press, 1942).
2. For some interesting exercises in releasing the breath see:
   Atme Richtig, Hiltrud Lodes (Munich: Ehrenwirth, 1977).
3. **Rebirthing in the New Age**, Sondra Ray and Leonard Orr (Milbrae: Celestial Arts).

CHAPTER V
INTEGRATING AND FINE TUNING BODYMIND

Basic body armor is released during the first stage of Postural Integration. This release may, of course, require more than the minimum seven sessions, but at some point a definite and remarkable phenomenon occurs: the body tissue becomes markedly softer, more consistent, resiliant, and also more malleable. This can be felt as one touches the structure -- from the outer tissue down to the deep. Even the tissue enveloping the intrinsic muscles is more available and responsive.

With this release the body begins to find new proportions. Wide hips become more narrow, small chests expand, torsos lengthen, faces relax, buttocks fill and round out. In some cases an individual may gain two inches in height and two inches in circumference around the chest. At the same time emotions and thoughts have become more flexible. One cries, laughs, sings, and groans more easily, and thoughts break free of their old limits.

Yet a problem remains. Although the client now feels more flexible, more alive, there may be some confusion in posture and behavior. The individual segments of the body have a greater range of movement, but although the pelvis, head, torso, arms, and legs turn and rock easily, they are not fully coordinated with each other. And emotionally and mentally there may be some confusion about what to do with this new freedom. The old center has been dissolved but a new one has not yet been found.

In working toward a new balance, in which energy flows but completes itself, we need to look at bodymind in terms of the parts of the self which need to come together, which need to harmonize and function with each other. And so during sessions 8, 9, and 10, the practitioner helps the individual to improve and maintain the unity of these aspects of bodymind: top and bottom, front and back, and left and right.

Also during sessions 8, 9 and 10 we need to emphasize the distinction made earlier between coarse and fine energy. On the one hand we go through very basic changes in our structure -- this is the reformation of our coarse energy. On the other hand, we can change very delicately, very subtly by adjusting the energy within the limits of the structure and character we have already developed, without altering their basic outlines. With integration there is an opportunity to use a great variety of fine tuning methods to stabilize our breathing, to distribute our energy, to harmonize and make us aware of our body movements, and to redirect our emotions and thoughts.

As we shall see in the final section of this chapter a special question arises about the use of fine tuning: how much should we focus our bodywork on the release of coarse armor, and how much on fine tuning the energy already present? This question is important not only in deciding when the final phase of integration begins, but also needs to be faced earlier during the process of release. If we focus too much on release, we do not allow enough time for far-reaching changes in an individual's structure to be accepted, to be assimilated as a part of a new way of being and behaving.

TOP AND BOTTOM
The Flowering of The Self

The two horizontal halves of our bodies are often very different. The upper half may be expanded and developed, while the lower half may be smaller and less developed. Or just the opposite may be the case: the upper half thin, small, maybe even collapsed, the lower broad, fleshy, and strong. This contrast is not merely a physical phenomenon, for our whole character is involved.(1) When we use one half of ourselves to manipulate the other half, as well as other people, we develop these top-heavy or bottom-heavy disproportions. As top-heavy we may be socially manipulative, but ungrounded. As bottom-heavy we may be seductive, but socially insecure.

By the integration stage these two halves are free of much of their armor but need to be coordinated with each other. When working with one half of bodymind the prac-

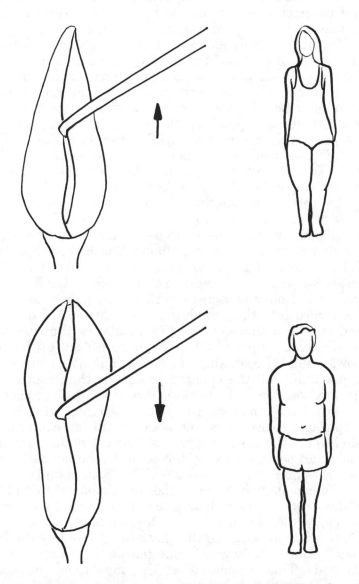

When the process of deep bodywork has reached the stage of integration -- sessions 8, 9, 10 -- the body can be likened to a flower bud whose petals are ready to open from the middle. If the top is still relatively tight, the petals are first opened upward in session 8. The next session, 9, then completes the opening. Session 10 encourages a harmonious balance throughout the whole, now completely open, structure.

titioner and client need to encourage movement, energy, and consciousness in the other half, to encourage a full upward and downward opening of the self.

Picture the body as an unopened flower bud. After the first stage of release, the petals are looser and ready to open, but either the lower or upper parts of the petals are more stuck. One strategy for starting the connecting or opening process is to work in one session on the half that is least ready to open, which is the half that still has comparatively more myofascial disorganization and restriction, as well as less emotional and mental consciousness. The freeing of this half of the body affects the other end of the petals in the other half as well.

In the accompanying diagram the top-heavy man provides an illustration of how his smaller, underdeveloped lower half needs to be opened first. The bottom-heavy woman provides an illustration of how her small, tight upper part needs to be opened first. I usually begin sessions 8 and 9 in the middle of the body at the level of the waist. If I have chosen to work on the lower half, I work downward into the remaining deep tensions of the pelvis and legs and thereby free fascial planes that allow the thoracic cage (upper half) to begin to lift out of the pelvis (lower half). Loosening the lower half helps unfold the upper half, and the opening process is then continued in the next session, 9, by working directly with the upper half.

But if the top of the flower bud is tighter, that is if the diaphragm, back, chest, or neck is still too contracted at the level of the deepest layers of fascia, I again start at the waist, but begin releasing the petals in the top half. In the next session I can then work with the bottom half.

We can change the metaphor for a moment to an image of the last chapter: the rib cage floating like a parachute above, while the pelvis and legs dangle below. In the illustration you can see the chest being lifted by the broad distribution of body weight and tension in the upper half of the body. This happens when the myofascial network of tissue is evenly distributed

Around the whole rib cage, taking pressure away from individual ribs or vertebrae. This even expansion above, in turn, promotes a descending flexibility in breathing and movement down through the belly, hips, sacrum, and legs.

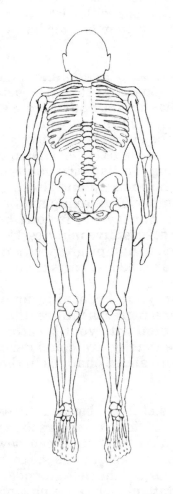

When the rib cage is free, it appears to float like a parachute, and the pelvis and legs lightly dangle below. The bodyweight is then evenly distributed throughout the structure and is supported by the myofascial (tissue) network, rather than bearing down on the spine, pelvis, and bones of the legs and feet.

It is worth noting that the bones are not the major support in an integrated body; but rather it is the fascia, when properly organized, which really bears the body weight. When the fascia is free, the bones move easily in fine, crisp articulations with each other.

To feel how the bottom and top halves can work together try the following:

Take a few deep breaths and notice the extent of your inhalations. How much do you expand in the chest and diaphragm, both in front and in back?

Stand with your legs apart. With the knees straight (to the extent possible) bend the upper half forward and down to the floor. Hang there with your arms dangling (perhaps the hands touch the floor) but do not bounce up and down. Imagine your hamstring muscles relaxing and lengthening. Be sure you do not try to lift your head. Hold this position for at least five minutes. Now slowly bring yourself back to an upright position. The head and upper back are the last parts to come to an upright position.

Examine your breathing again. Does your thorax expand more? Is the breathing in your chest more connected with your breathing in the lower back? Notice that by stretching the back of the legs you can bring about changes in the upper part of your body.

As the planes of fascia between the two halves begin to connect, we also begin to open ourselves to more integrated ways of feeling and thinking. I can now say to myself, "I am expansive above and at the same time I can support myself below." Or, "I am well grounded, and I can soar." When we integrate ourselves we no longer use one part to manipulate or compensate for another part of ourselves. We begin to realize that we can have both without competition.

Of course not everybody falls into the category of top-heavy or bottom-heavy. But the above strategy can be easily modified. We can start in the middle of the body and in one session work both upward and downward, then in the next sesion continue toward the extremities, working with the head and arms above and the legs and feet below. We are still opening the flower petals, but gradually in both directions.

Now that the petals of the flower bud (the client's body) are opening along their whole length, session 10 can begin with the feet and proceed selectively toward the head, balancing the front and back, and left and right of bodymind.

FRONT AND BACK

Expanding Around The Self

We also divide ourselves from front to back. We hunch, curl forward, contracting the belly, protecting our hearts, guts, and genitals. Or we rear back our shoulders, thrusting our chests out to meet adversity, while our backs and asses remain well-protected. Notice how either your front or back half is less conscious, more deadened to what's happening around you. We sit in the front or the back of rooms; we plunge head-long into our projects or hold back; we sleep in a foetal position or laid out like someone being crucified. It is convenient to handle the world with our customary attitudes, but in the process we manipulate ourselves.

Above I stated that the balancing of front and back (and left and right) is selective. It is essential when shifting deep layers of tissue to work carefully and thoroughly with the myofascial disorganization around and between over-contracted muscle groups. Care needs to be taken not to work too much with the tissue of weaker, opposing groups.

Take for example the person curled forward. If the flexor groups of the belly and anterior shoulders (which pull him or her into such a protected position) are very strong and need to be lengthened, the opposing extensors of the back are slack and need strengthening, not by deep work but by gentle guidance. The person who thrusts forward in front, likewise may need deep work to relieve the contractions in the back of the body, and gentle tuning on the open front of the body. We shall see in the next section that fine tuning techniques can help to wake up these weak structures.

It is possible as we deal with the front-back (as well as top-bottom, and left-right) relationships within our structures that we find ourselves balanced in one part but not in another. To continue with the example: the person who leans over backward (to help someone) is hyperextending toward the back, that is, the back muscles are overcontracted. This is the case in the upper body, but in the lower body the front of the thighs may be the muscles which are overcontracted. One part of the person, the upper part, is moving away from the person to be "helped," while another part, the lower, is moving toward the person. Selective work is, then, not just work with the front or back, it is work which follows the particular needs and patterns of the individual.

When front and back begin to function together as a unit we can begin to affirm the fact that our consciousness goes all the way around us, that we radiate our energy in all directions. We can say, "I am open in front, without closing myself behind." Or "I allow the world to view me from behind as I meet the world in front."

Try out the following in a large empty auditorium or church. If these are not available imagine the whole scene.

The auditorium is filled with hundreds of people. When your name is called, you are sitting on the back row and you have to walk along the aisle to the front. Walk slowly and feel the crowd turning to look at you and continuing to look at you after you have gone past them. Mount the stage in front and stand before an enormous mirror which reflects you and the crowd. With your back still to the crowd, you then announce to their clapping and cheering, "I am what I am both in front and in back."

When I recognize that my balance depends on the acceptance of every side of my experience, I can also allow myself to focus on the front of myself, knowing that as my energy moves and changes in its continuous cycle, I can also in another moment focus on the back of myself.

RIGHT AND LEFT

Balancing Masculine and Feminine

If we look at the human cortex's function in controlling the sides of our bodies and personalities, we find that the usually more dominant left hemisphere controls the right side of the body, along with such analytic functions as calculation and linguistic naming. The usually less dominant right hemisphere controls the left side of the body, along with such functions as sensing wholistic forms, making metaphoric connections, and creating musical patterns. My experience leads me to postulate that our extrinsic, goal oriented outer behavior is under the power of the analytic, left hemisphere, while inner, gestalting, intrinsic behavior is closer to the intuitive right hemisphere.(2)

It is not surprising, considering that the majority of humanity is right handed, to find that the right half of the body is more developed in size and strength than the left. This is a form of extrinsic power and awareness on the outside of the body. In these right-handed individuals the intrinsic (inner) muscles on the right side have been overwhelmed by the extrinsics.

Although the left side is weaker on the outside, its intrinsic muscles are usually better developed. This may seem surprising, since our left-sided movements often seem awkward. But this awkwardness happens because we try to initiate our external behavior with the weak extrinsic muscles of the left side. We can, in fact, gracefully use the left side intrinsics to balance our right sided extrinsic movements. When we throw a ball or swing a tennis racquet with the right side, the left side provides a balancing follow-through.

In contrast, left side dominant persons have generally better developed intrinsics on both sides, especially on the left side. This gives them an advantage in initiating movement and maintaining stability, but if they have not developed ambidexterity they often lack the more assertive character of very right-sided persons.

I am not just considering physical movements. The very right-sided person may be competitive and goal oriented, while the left-sided person is often more intuititive and artistic. I have found that when I begin to release the armor of right-sided individuals, there can be an initial confusion in customary habits and movements. They stumble and miss their goals, because beneath the overdeveloped right side there is usually little intrinsic stability. When I release the armor of the left side dominant individuals, they do not normally experience a loss of intrinsic stability, but they often begin to show a surprisingly aggressive part of themselves.

What is evident in both cases is a confrontation between the active-receptive, masculine-feminine sides of ourselves. While working toward the integration of these aspects of bodymind, I have found it extremely effective to use a two-sided approach. I work on both sides of the body (mind) simultaneously or alternatively, in different yet complimentary ways. We are often stuck directing our energy along one path to the exclusion of the other, because we do not accept the possibility that right and left, active and passive, masculine and feminine can function harmoniously together.

Here is an exercise you may have played with in childhood:

> **Try writing your signature backward (mirror image) from right to left with the hand which you do not normally use for signing. Notice any feelings of confusion, frustration, or surrender which may surface. Try now to sign with both hands simultaneously. The little used hand signs as above and the other hand signs normally. Notice how one hand may help the other. Try the mirror signature again alone and see if it is easier. Try your normal signature alone. Has it changed?**

In working with right side dominant persons I may with one hand press deep into the right side to free and activate bound and inactive intrinsic muscles,while with the other hand interact with the outer, extrinsic structures of the left side. This cross-over, along with a coordination of inside and outside, helps to furnish energy just where right-sided persons have neglected their feelings and awareness.

Denise fences three times a week at her sport club in Montreal. During the first seven sessions, I concentrated on releasing the huge overdeveloped extrinsic muscles of her right thigh and right half of her abdomen and waist. I had also, in sessions 8 and 9 started to help her connect her heavy bottom with her smaller top half.

Then during the 8th session I felt we needed to make contact with her weaker left side. I had her reverse her normal fencing position such that she could thrust with the left side, while I hooked the fingers of one of my hands into the attachments of the left psoas, on the inner thigh, and the fingers of my other hand into the attachments of her right rectus femoris on the front of the other thigh.

She felt weak and confused as she moved but suddenly realized how much of her attention and feeling she had put into outer defensive and offensive maneuvers, and how she had lost contact with a subtler energy needed to move back and forth between passivity and activity.

With left side dominant persons I find it may be important to concentrate an entire session of integrative work exclusively on the neglected right side of the body, encouraging them to experiment with broad, active, outer movements and feelings.

Charles was called "Charlie the Chinaman" because of his left-handed dexterity. He was a graceful dancer, a gifted pianist, and great cook. But he was shy. He rarely shared these talents with his friends. During the final integrating sessions, I worked with the large outer muscles of his left side - - triceps, chest muscle, thigh, and calf. While

pinching and poking these muscles, I encouraged him to swing and kick at me with his right arm and leg. At first he felt confused, but soon started to relish these aggressive movements.

But a two-sided approach to integration offers more than work with the neglected side of bodymind. It is also a way of helping clients feel the harmony of what they often consider to be conflicting opposites. When, for example, I feel the pain that deep tissue work may evoke, and at the same time I feel the gentleness and caring touch of the practitioner, my old attitudes -- if I feel pain I am being victimized or if I cry I won't be accepted as masculine -- are swept away. Two-sided work recognizes the possibility of escaping from these kinds of double binds and allowing our feelings and thoughts to become more whole. (3)

FINE TUNING

Refining Without Controlling

Integration has been explained as a process in which we allow the parts of ourselves to find a unity and balance. This integration (as well as release) can be either "coarse" or "fine." When I work to change my general bodymind posture -- my sway back, my hysterical fear, my schizoid tendency to analyze everything --I am focusing on "coarse" energy. Here I am concerned with large blocks of energy, with deeply ingrained habits, which set the basic directions of my life. On the other hand, I can stay within the limits of my general bodymind attitude, and without trying to change my sway back, fear, or my intellectual penchant, I can refine and improve the circulation of the patterns already present. I am in this case working with "fine" energy.

The stage of releasing armor is mostly "coarse" work. As armor is released, the body shape and quality of our emotions and thoughts are radically altered. But during release we also need some fine tuning. We need time and space to assimilate the changes we are undergoing, even if the recentering of ourselves is only temporary until more armor begins to crumble.

When individuals go through changes such as a greatly expanded chest, lengthened torso, slimmer hips, more flexible knees and ankles, they frequently experience some disorientation, an occasional loss of balance, and some emotional confusion. I then find it helpful to slow the process of transformation by giving fewer sessions and working more with fine energy. Fine work is also needed as a preparation for coarse work. During each session of work, I use gentle movement awareness, acupressure points, etc. to help the client prepare to confront coarse armor and to flow with its release.

On the other hand, much of integrating work is a fine tuning of what has already happened in the releasing stage of the process. Yet there are also general coarse transformations during integration. As we experience the freedom and power in allowing each side of us -- top and bottom, front and back, left and right -- to function together, our physical and psychic dimensions may also be radically altered.

Finally, however, we need to emphasize, not coarse change, but fine tuning in order to establish harmonious, stable patterns for future transformation. As we shall see in the next secton it is not always easy to decide when more coarse or more fine work is needed.

What is especially important in all fine tuning is an attitude of not deliberately trying to change oneself. In fine tuning we have a general direction in which we want to move, a context in which we move comfortably, but we have no specific destination, no exact goal for our changes. Fine changes call for an open-ended, spontaneous process of which we are mindful, attentive, meditative, but which we do not try to manipulate or control. I have found four areas of fine tuning especially useful in deep bodywork: breath regulation, energy distribution, movement awareness, and psychological redirection.

We have already seen in the previous chapter how breathing is integrating when it flows freely through a cycle of charge and discharge, and recharge. In working to fine tune this breathing cycle, the practitioner helps the client sustain a meditative attitude throughout a variety of breaths -- rapid, slow, even, uneven. By watching the breathing we realize that we can always return to a point where we can choose to follow, as our needs dictate, a given kind of breath, without controlling it. We can become excited in our breathing, but see that we can and will return to a calmer rhythm. We can also play with expanding our breath along with large actions of the extrinsic, outside muscles and watch how we can quietly contract our breath with inner intrinsic movements. As we watch our expansion and contraction we flow with it.

Let's now look at energy regulation. I have also mentioned in the previous chapter how acupressure, using the circular flow of the five elements, can help us toward balance. Fine tuning with the five elements is not so much helping an individual find new energy or to get rid of excessive energy. It is rather the delicate distribution of energy throughout Water, Wood, Fire, Earth and Metal. Using acupuncture points to regulate this flow requires receptivity and consciousness. I look at my client's excessive fear and see that I can with the help of various points begin to allow this build-up of Water (fear) energy to spill over into Wood (anger). My client already has this energy. I need only encourage it to follow its natural course.

Or in another case -- after working deep on the muscles of the jaw (masseter, temporalis) my client may begin to experience lots of held-back anger, but may become uncontrolled or excessive in its expression. By working with Earth, the meridians of receptivity, I can draw off this sudden, new excess of anger and help my client be more sympathetic, more open.

In several styles of working to make us more aware of our movements -- Alexander Technique, Feldenkrais Method, and Aston Patterning -- we find recogniton of a meditative and watchful but non-interfering attitude. In the Alexander Technique we hold empty zen-like images which we repeat but do not try to execute. "Let the neck be free to let the head go forward and up, while the back lengthens and broadens," is a classic Alexander image and formula which guides but does not follow the habitual goals we have built into our posture over the years. In

Feldenkrais the different parts of the body are given an opportunity to communicate with each other without the usual habitual commands. In stretching and exploring one side of my body I am already communicating, if my controlling consciousness does not interfere, with the other side of my body, and if my right arm moves more easily my left begins to recognize this and respond more freely as well. Or in Aston Patterning we are encouraged to find simple lines of symmetric movement, which we can explore by coordinating our whole body.

Many bodyworkers who specialize in these kinds of soft, delicate movements, which also are often accompanied by light manipulations of the body, object to deep tissue work, seeing it as counter-productive. They see deep work as not only unnecessarily painful, but actually provoking deep resistance of bodymind -- causing a tightening of the core.

I feel two points of clarificaton are important. First, careful deep tissue work is always within the limits of what clients can accept, and thus gives them an opportunity to become more aware of what is already present in the tissues. Of course, if bodywork is too fast, or too abrupt, then armor is activated rather than being dissolved. Secondly, working deep is compatible with very gentle guidance of the body.

For example, in reaching toward the deepest layers of tissue along the spine, the practitioner will often encounter hard, well-developed strands of the sacrospinalis. Any attempt to force one's way through this mass to reach the tissue which lies underneath (e.g. the multifidus which spans the vertebral processes and executes small, intrinsic movements of the spine and ribs) would evoke a great deal of pain, perhaps creating intense protective spasms in the back.

One way to work deeply, yet gently, with this area is to use one hand to press an individual rib gently inward. This pressure gives a message to the muscles of the back, both the outer sacrospinalis as well as the deeper multifidus, that their job has been taken over for them and they can relax. At this moment the practitioner can use his other hand (fingertips or knuckles) to penetrate slowly to the deepest intrinsic musculature and reorganize hitherto unavailable tissue. At the same time light breath

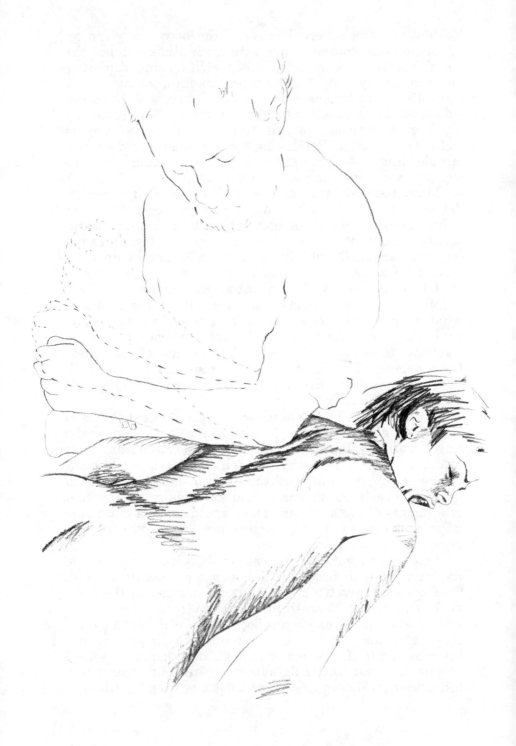

work and imagery help the client assimilate the changes taking place. Gentle movement awareness, then, need not be thought of as work that is different and separate from deep tissue work.

Perhaps these methods of movement awareness are such effective ways of fine tuning the bodymind because they give an opportunity to the nervous system to reorient itself. We saw in previous chapters how, according to one wholistic interpretation, the gates in certain parts of the nervous system can be said to be set by previous painful experience, set by a protective armor which freezes the tissue in and around the muscles. As deep tissue is moved and freed, we relive and accept the event, gaining a new consciousness of the way we have previously set these gates. Now in fine tuning bodymind, we are able to begin resetting the gates for new kinds of experience which involve the whole nervous system.

According to the gate theory, the nervous system is a reciprocal unity, with changes in any one part of it affecting every other part. All nervous activity is, then, not directly controlled by the brainstem, but the lower centers help activate other parts of the system. The way I am setting the gates (rearranging them) in any given part of my system is helping to rearrange the gates in other parts of my system. During the fine tuning work of Postural Integration, then, the possibilities for new movements (feelings and thoughts) are enormously enlarged. My movement is not narrowly dependent on my old armored patterns of brain conditioned response, but is open to all the arrangements (of the gates) which my nervous system can make with itself.

Jim was a member of the Hell's Angels motorcycle gang near San Francisco until he was shot from behind in the head. Since part of his right brain was destroyed, he had very little movement or feeling in the left side of his body. From the beginning of the sessions he felt good about the passive mobility I was helping him create in the joints which had become stiff from inactivity. After I had softened every major segment of his body, I began exploring ways of connecting his still active

154

side with the paralyzed side. As I worked simultaneously on both sides, some of the muscles in
his left side twitched and he had the beginning of
new sensations. I now had him use his right side
as much as possible but at the same time forming
images of how his left side was connected to his
right.

Finally there is the psychological side to our fine
tuning. Another area of fine tuning is the harmonizing
and directing of our thoughts and feelings, what has
generally become the province of psychotherapy and
psychiatry. One difficulty that arises in these therapies is
that there is a tendency to overtune one part of the self. By
concentrating on fine work to the exclusion of coarse work
on the basic body structure, the therapist and client may
become lost in working with words or ideas. Of course
psychological work can enrich the process of transformation as recognized by Andreas Vontobel, a psycho-
analyst and Postural Integrator in Zurich. He gives the
following example:

> Miriam had been anxious and morbid most of
> her life. She was afraid to come out of her dark,
> damp cellar room. Her stiff, emaciated body
> emitted a foul, putrid smell. In her dreams she was
> invariably overwhelmed and trapped by un-
> controllable powers. Giant sized, domestic cats
> commandeered her automobile while she, tiny and
> afraid, looked on from the rear seat. During the
> first years of analysis, she remained stuck in the
> same patterns of powerlessness and fear.
> A few days after Andreas started deep tissue
> work with her, she had several dreams of deep
> incisions which painfully exposed her insides. But
> the pain she started to recognize -- from her mother,
> who had often beaten her -- was now experienced
> and shared in the context of Andreas' nourishment
> and guidance. Her body softened and greatly
> expanded, and her dreams changed. She now saw
> herself walking through beautiful gardens safely
> accompanied by tigers, lions, and bears.

Andreas was now able to help her begin to see her beauty and strength and the process of analysis soon reached a satisfying resolution with her beginning a new profession and becoming engaged to be married.

In discussing "The Experience of Release" (Chapter III) I showed how a gestalt or zen attitude toward our bodyminds helps us to claim fully alienated parts of ourselves. These methods help us not only to claim parts -- unconscious back, stiff knees -- by becoming these parts -- e.g. "I am my back and I demand attention" -- but also to explore a consciousness which is more global. I go further than just being there in one part of my self. As a unified and continuous self, I flow from moment to moment. I can enter into an exchange, a dialogue with the other aspects of myself. I am both my top and bottom half and I give energy to both halves. As a unified self, I have the power to choose without conflict. I can now hate my father; I can now love him.

The condition of this kind of integration is the acceptance, during release of my armor, of previously foreign aspects of myself, but the integraton itself is more than acceptance, it is a flowing, unified, stream of choosing and discovering what I want and need.

Another way of redirecting our emotions and thoughts is to fine tune them with affirmations. Affirmations, when they remain open-ended and are not attempts to manipulate ourselves, are ways for us to claim the power that has been released by the crumbling of our past armor. Whenever I repeat to myself, "I am opening myself to the love of other people," my affirmation is broad enough to give me a direction for change. But when I say "I can get Mary to love me," I am manipulating and armoring myself.

Affirmations are powerful means for fine tuning ourselves, if they are not substitutes for dealing with the frustrations of life. An affirmation gives a context and direction for change, if we have already allowed our fear, rage, and sadness to be expressed and claim it as a part of us. But if our affirmations are simply means to overcome so-called "negative" feelings, we have made ourselves unconscious for the sake of the false promise of an affirmation. "I am joyful and happy" is an appropriate affirmation only if we also allow ourselves, when the occasion arises, to fully experience our sadness.

When integration and fine tuning have been fully effective, a major transformation has taken place in bodymind (see the accompanying before and after photographs), a transformation which, in one sense, is permanent: the person can never completely return to a heavily armored, unconscious conditon. Of course, with accidents and stress, integrated and fine tuned individuals may lose part of their balance, but with only minimal further work with themselves, they can easily recover their balance.

Also for those individuals who specialize in refining their energy, I have developed an advanced type of Postural Integration in which I work with the innermost, residual core, balancing the delicate energy which lies deep at the attachments of our intrinsic muscles (on the skeleton) with the outer energy of our large, but now soft, extrinsic muscles.

FINE TUNING AND THE LIMITS OF CHANGE
Posture Versus Flexibility

During my visits to Die Alte Pinakothek in Munich, I have been struck by the energetic vitality of Ruben's nude female figures. The art historian Von Bode describes them as beautiful heroines "with their soft skin and their blood, which pulsating with excitement ..., reddens their cheeks and flushes their bodies with rich tones of color." (4) On the one hand these figures seem to be good examples of the free flowing energy of finely tuned bodies. Yet on the other hand, most of these nudes have overarched backs and knotted, tightened buttocks, which according to our bodywork principles, would block the free flow of energy. We ask the question, then, whether creating a fine balance of our energy is really independent from improving our basic (coarse) posture and attitudes. Why try to help a person change his sway back, if he can be full of energy and vitality just as he is? Stanley Keleman raises a similar question when he writes:

> **Civilization has allowed some of us to become artists and poets, to assert our existence in very soft ways. This means that the effort to construct an ideal male or female body is only a hidden orthodoxy. That is why I disapprove of the single postural ideal set up by the Alexander method or Ida Rolf's work. If we say that the male pelvis must thrust forward in a penetrating manner or it will be lacking in masculine aggressiveness and sexual pleasure, we have a new kind of chauvinism. This does not respect the individual differences in body types and life styles. (5)**

Practitioners of the Alexander method and Rolfing might reply that they do not seek to impose an ideal but only want to help the individual equalize opposing muscular forces in the body. The pelvis, they might say, without being forced, then naturally moves into efficient and aligned position. "Thrusting" the pelvis forward would be contrary to this idea of natural and conscious balance.

Yet Keleman still has a point. As I see it, even the ideal of a relaxed and balanced body may in some cases be an imposition. For example, when I am working with individuals with severe lordosis (overarched lower back), the whole structure, including the basic skeletal growth, has developed around swaying their backs. Thus the question that arises for me is just how much can the coarse overall structure change in the direction of relaxed alignment?

My feeling is that I alone cannot answer this question for my clients and that there is a process of discovery as they seek to release their armor. They can ask themselves whether the time, energy, and emotional and psychological upheaval required for further alignment of the pelvis is more important than fine tuning -- looking for more streaming, more refinement of their energy within the general limits of a still swayed posture. Of course, where there is a decision to focus on fine rather than coarse energy, there may be some coarse changes: the chest may expand, the buttocks soften, the legs straighten, even while the fundamental sway stubbornly remains.

In individuals where the coarse structure does radically alter, where the pelvis does become free enough to move toward effortless alignment, fine energy has even more possibilities for being regulated. There is, though, often the problem of maintaining such a delicate balance between our coarse and fine energy. We may feel overwhelmed by the energy available to us. One typical defensive pattern for dealing with the high levels of energy which well up inside us, when our bodies begin to become better aligned, is to revert to some old armored physical posture in order to handle the flood of feelings and thoughts; or to revert to some neutral emotional state in order to be able to focus on the newly discovered, delicate balance of bodymind.

Of course each person must discover the degree of energetic freedom and gravitational balance which he or she can simultaneously tolerate. And at times we may not choose to accept fully the intensity, the consequences of complete body alignment and flexibility. Perhaps the plump, rolling, fleshy sexuality of the Ruben's nudes is in part gained by their overeagerness outwardly to surrender, while at the same time they are still inwardly holding back, conserving their energy.

We have seen in this chapter that the integration and fine tuning of bodymind call for a variable approach to our complex sensory, intellectual, emotional and somatic lives. Both the practitioner and client are participating in a dynamic transformation, that is at once science, living sculpture, therapy, and love. In the next chapter we shall look at how the practitioner and client can be in a constant, flowing interaction.

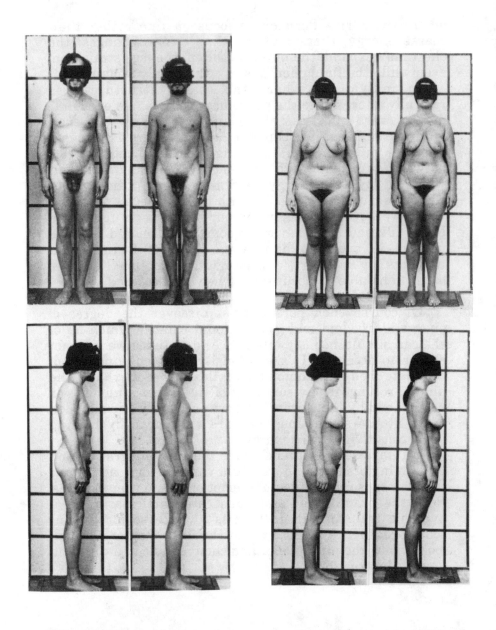

These before and after photographs show how two individuals changed during ten sessions of Postural Integration. Note how the bodies became longer, more symmetrical and more upright. As persons they also became softer, more open and more expressive.

FOOTNOTES FOR CHAPTER V

1. See both:
   The Body Reveals, op.cit.
   Bodymind, op.cit.
2. "How The Split Brain Gets a Joke," Howard Gardener, **Psychology Today,** Feb. 1981, pp. 74-78.
3. **Steps To an Ecology of Mind,** Gregory Bateson (New York: Chandler, 1972).
4. **Alte Pinakothek Muenchen** (Munich: Wasterman, 1976).
5. **Voices and Visions,** Sam Keen (New York: Harper and Row, 1974) p. 162.

CHAPTER VI

BETWEEN YOU AND ME
SHARING AND TRANSFORMING BODYMIND

In the books **The Myth of Mental Illness** and **Sex by Prescription**, (1) Thomas Szasz has deftly exposed how some physicians and therapists impose their diagnoses on their patients, not just by misdiagnosis, but also by invention of the disease, itself. Bodyworkers also run the risk of imposing their ideas, feelings, and the sheer force of their physical bodies on their clients. Equally clients run the risk of wanting to be cured by the manipulations of the practitioner, rather than through their own self-awareness.

On the one hand, practitioners need to refrain from intimidating clients with statements about their condition and what they need to change. If I tell you that you are a "masochist" or "burdened" and that you need to experience only very soft ways of contacting other people and I hesitate to work deep in your structure, this advice and approach may well be irrelevant to the hidden anger you want to express, and even disruptive to the process of your transformation. And if you the client, come asking for relief from your insecurity, you may succeed in eliciting from me a sympathy which will not contribute to your need to stay with, and work through, your chronic fears.

On the other hand, if I do hold back my attitude and restrain from acting on intuitions about how your bodymind can be reshaped, I may repress myself and fail to share what is actually valuable for your growth. Many people have over-inflated or depreciated views of themselves, and may need to be awakened by another perspective. If I see you as having basically a thin, fragile structure with little muscular development but you want very much to become a bodyworker, do I discourage you from what I see as a futile attempt to develop the power needed to perform the physical aspects of this type of work, and instead encourage you to find a less demanding way of expressing yourself physically? And are you, the client, to be less expressive of your needs in order to begin taking more responsibility for yourself? But who am I to set what may seem to be your obvious limit? And who are you to limit yourself? After all, isn't healing an attempt to offer the possibility of changing what appears to be our limits?

In order to find a way out of this dilemma we need to first recognize that all healing is a reciprocal act, an intimate inner and outer contact between the practitioner and individual. Both are taking part in an event which leads toward the balancing of the other's energy -- a balance which encourages change and flow of our physical, emotional and mental experience. When the nature of this reciprocity between the practitioner and individual is understood, we can then see that the individual is free to express, discover, and heal him or herself without outside control and manipulation, and that at the same time, the practitioner cannot be a neutral observer.

In effective healing practitioners are there to give of themselves -- their physical force, information, and feelings. We shall see that the direction, power, and limits of an individual's bodymind transformation emerge from what happens in the exchange between both practitioner and individual.

RECIPROCITY THROUGH INNER AND OUTER CONTACT
Dance and Dancer As One

Many students of bodywork initially have the idea that if they learn exactly where in the anatomical structure they can make a certain type of hand, finger, or elbow manipulation, they can, with some practice, master the complexities of deep tissue work. Actually no amount of observation, study, or practice -- although important -- can substitute for the need to make contact with an individual through an inner attitude. When I, as practitioner, begin with inner sensitivity, all my movements, all my contact with the other person, are both receptive and initiating -- receptive in that I allow my force to adjust to the resistance or openness of the individual, initiating in that I take the individual beyond the limits of his or her armor.

164

Consider what happens when I, the practitioner, or you, the individual with whom I'm working, make contact only externally or superficially. If I push against you with an outer effort alone, then I cannot easily regulate -- increase, diminish, change -- my force. You would feel my hands unresponsive to your inner needs and defend yourself with your outside armor. Since my effort may be too fast, too deep, too hard, or just the opposite, too slow, etc., you would either become tense or totally passive in your extrinsic musculature. There is, then, no real contact, only an outer clash or compromise. This kind of outer contact, not real touching and caring, simply reinforces our armor. I am dumping on you my old feelings of power, while you are using my assault on your outside armor to reinforce old patterns of self-defense.

Sometimes the practitioner and client begin their contact with careful intrinsic movements but then fail to follow through with complete external contact. If we begin together and I apply pressure so carefully that I adjust to every move I sense you making, I have only followed your needs without helping you discover new possibilities beyond your armor. Similarly if you submit inwardly to all my initiatives, you never discover your external power to give and interact.

In contrast to these incomplete attempts, full contact between you, the client, and me, the practitioner, is a special inner and outer reciprocity, a sharing in which we respect each other. Just as I move with, and yet guide, your inner and outer energy, you do not react, but dance with my pressure. This is a dance in which the dancer and the dance become one. It is a unifying movement of both of us, without action or reaction, only a simultaneity like the moves of opposing tai chi partners.

Try the following:

Stand facing a partner of approximately equal size and weight. With your knees and toes pointed toward each other hold on to each other's hands with double grips. Lean backward, with the feet still in place, until your arms are stretched straight and you support each other's weight. Holding this balance, bend at the knees and squat and return to

an upright position. Try the same, holding only one hand. Did you notice, a fine point of balance which freed both of you to move easily? Did you find that trying too hard destroyed the balance between you?

It may seem that the exchange cannot be equal. After all, you have come to me for help. How can you participate as an equal partner, if part of your armor is a defense against just such an exchange of energy, a resistance at some deep level to the possibility of your own self-transformation? Even if I am centered and initiate my force from inside, and make sensitive, respectful contact with you, but you are afraid to surrender, how can the dance even begin?

For there to be a beginning in the healing process we need to recognize that both of us are incomplete in a paradoxical sense. You are resistant to change; that is the nature of armor. Yet you are willing to give up that armor when you are shown a possible path for change. I expect you to change. I want to help you overcome your blocks, yet I need to be very flexible, to change directions, if the direction I have suggested is not effective.

In my role as healer, as Postural Integrator, I cannot completely accept your armored past. I work on the narrow border between imposing myself on you and accommodating myself to your old, armored games. The deep work with your tissue, blocked feelings and thoughts, elicits both pain and pleasure and is also a contact in which we feel resistance and release. If my force is too great or too painful for you, I will cut off the possibility of you beginning your own transformation process and healing. If my force is too weak or accommodating, I give up my power as healer.

Ron Kurtz and I are in slight disagreement about how the practitioner enters into this relationship. In his **Training Manual**, which I highly recommend, Ron writes that "The best thing you can do is to be totally accepting. If you can be loving, accepting, nonjudgmental, the person is going to feel safe." (2) He also writes, "Never work against anyone's will or wishes. You must avoid setting off the defense systems."(3) I have seen Ron work beautifully in this gentle, safe way, helping many individuals through really difficult blocks. I have also found it extremely helpful to work in this way.

Yet sometimes there are clients who use the practitioner's gentleness as a way of avoiding confrontation with deep-seated anger, fear, or sorrow. At one level the client wants me to be gentle so as to help keep our space safe, but at another level there is a deep need to resolve explosive feelings. I feel that sometimes confrontations are necessary in which the practitioner demands change -- perhaps even with physical anger -- in order to help break through this armor. Confrontation is risky because the acceptable limits are not defined, and it is possible to lose a client or friend, if you go too far. But life does not always have clear limits, and transformation is not always possible in a **totally** safe environment.

Establishing and maintaining a delicately balanced exchange between the practitioner and individual calls for a variety of approaches and methods. Free, spontaneous breathing is essential to the cyclic balance of our energy, and when both the practitioner and client share and explore patterns of breathing in unison with each other, they are better able to sense the give and take needed in healing. All the integrating and fine tuning techniques which I use help maintain this sensitive exchange.

This exchange allows for and encourages the direct expression of emotions arising from either practitioner or client. When I work with you, my role is to encourage you to explore the feelings that arise with the release of tensions you hold in your body, to confront and work through your unfinished business, and also to help you realize what you feel here and now about me. I need to give you my feelings of satisfaction, frustration, and sympathy. In this sharing it is not my job to remain emotionally neutral or objective; but rather to give of myself and at the same time allow you the freedom not to live up to my expectations about how you can transform yourself.

The bodyworker and individual should both be free to project their needs on the other and to reject and accept the roles in which they are cast by each other. I am your parent; you are my child. I refuse to be your parent; you refuse to be my child. In the process of psychoanalysis the patient may slowly, over a period of perhaps months or years, transfer his or her parental needs upon the analyst, and thereafter gradually free him or herself from this transference. In the process of wholistic bodywork (through direct and deep transformation of bodymind structures), we are continually and simultaneously both forming and breaking the transference. Of course, some period of time may also be needed for the integration and assimilation of this dual freedom into an individual's life.

Hans, who was introduced in Chapter II, had come to me for six sessions. He had begun to understand how his resistance to his father had been a way of covering up his loneliness, emptiness, and vulnerability, but at one level, he still cast me in the role of his father, as the instrument of his own pain and suffering. In the seventh session, the opening of the heavy armor of the head and neck, I encouraged him to go further into this attitude toward his father but to direct it towards me. At the height of his rage, as I finished working around his thick jaw muscles, I shared with him that I could play a fatherly role sometimes, but that right now I wasn't going to be treated as his father, that I accepted his anger but that I also liked his soft vulnerable side. This was confusing for him, but at this point we both started to find a new dimension in our friendship.

STRATEGIES OF INTERACTION WITH ONE OR MORE PRACTITIONERS
Giving In To The Whole Gang

We saw in Chapter III that although the work during the first phases of wholistic bodywork is focused on the outer extrinsic structure, the inner structure of the individual needs to begin to open as well. In later phases, the focus shifts to inner structures, but with work on the outside shell remaining important to the complete release of armor. The whole process of exchange between the practitioner and individual is, then, a gradual opening of the individual from outside toward inside and inside toward outside. The practitioner is both leading and following in the dance. He or she does not need to know exactly the direction the dance will take or where it may end; only to be grounded enough to initiate and receive movement, force, and weight in the center of the pelvis, which is sometimes called the hara.

When the practitioner interacts with an individual, this low center of gravity, where we hold our gut consciousness, is coordinated below with bending knees and grounded feet, and above with shoulders anchored by gentle action of the muscles of the mid-back (lower rhomboids). This stance resembles what the Alexander teachers call the monkey. It is also similar to the grounded movements of tai chi -- with a slight variation. The practitioner ideally shifts his or her whole center forward to engage the individual's resistance, but not to a point where the practitioner's balance is lost or the client does not have space to maneuver.

The client, on the other hand, cannot be too active or passive. In the release and integration of myofascial structures (and other aspects of bodymind), the interactive role of the individual is to gently squirm, to find, confront, and explore the unconscious areas of tissue. The client does not just lie down to have the work done, he or she may stand, sit, roll, reach out, stretch, contract, or relax, all of which is to be accompanied by charging and discharging breath, feeling, and thought.

One of the most powerful experiences in the wholistic bodywork process is the phenomenon of several practitioners working simultaneously on one individual. The power of this group work is not only that different parts of an individual's body are simultaneously brought into coordinated change, but also that conflicting emotions and attitudes aroused by different practitioners, working together, gives the individual an opportunity to resolve persistent, partly unconscious conflicts.

Let's first take the experience of simultaneous change in different body segments. If, for example, one practitioner works inside the abdominal cavity with the psoas, another with the neck, and a third with the back, it is possible, with sensitive cooperation of the group, to achieve rapid integrative changes throughout the length of the entire body, simultaneous changes which would be difficult to accomplish with only one practitioner. Moreover, during the initial stage of bodywork, after the release of separate segments (legs, head, etc.), some individuals, though freer, still have difficulty functioning as a unified whole.

For example, when a freed pelvis flattens, the head may shift forward. Or when the head shifts into a free and posterior position, the lumbar area may shorten and the back sway. However, if several practitioners simultaneously engage all these segments, the individual may experience a wholeness and completeness that was elusive in the separate work. This simultaneity is also possible when several practitioners work together on both the inside and outside of an individual.

There is a second dimension to this type of group work. Different parts of the body hold different emotions which may be in conflict. In my life I have often felt weak and vulnerable, and on the other hand, I have felt a great deal of anger and impatience. I had not, however, fully connected these divergent feelings and so had not experienced them as a unified part of myself. This was resolved during a session of Postural Integration being given to me.

While one practitioner worked with the vulnerability I felt in my belly, another practitioner provoked the anger held in my jaws. My experience of these two strong unresolved feelings at the same time allowed me to see that I had used my anger as a delayed reaction to my feelings of hurt and rejection. I saw that my anger can be a powerful and immediate way of dealing with what I want but am not getting.

Another powerful aspect of the emotional dimension in group work is that one practitioner can be the instrument of deep painful release, while another makes soft, nurturing contact. This contrasting, dual experience can help the client understand how pain need not always be negative. Again, in my own experience, as one practitioner worked deep with the armor around my eyes and helped me re-experience my childhood sadness of being abandoned, another practitioner gently caressed my torso and rocked me in her arms. I was then able to experience my sadness without feeling abandoned.

I call this type of work "paradoxical," because the deep and soft, painful and pleasurable are experienced together. In paradoxical work the practitioner often acts as an archetype of male and female forces, in a kind of primal family therapy. As we have earlier seen, paradoxical work can also be used on opposite halves of the body to help integrate the left and right brain hemispheres, as well as to resolve conflicts between bottom and top, and front and back.

Here is a group exercise:

Sit in the middle of a circle with several friends around you. Assign each a role: father, mother, sister, brother, teacher, lover, etc. Begin talking about one of your most difficult problems. Have each of your friends give you advice according to their roles. As the drama continues, experience and express feelings as completely as possible. It may help if your friends give their advice as a chorus. They should give both positive and negative advice, sometimes quietly, sometimes forcefully. When you reach a point of exhaustion, relax and let them all massage you gently.

BODYMIND TYPES AND THE LIMITS OF CHANGE
Guiding Without Classifying

When healing change is seen as a reciprocal exchange between practitioner and individual, the dilemma we faced at the beginning of this chapter is resolved. When I give my force, feelings, and ideas to you from a receptive and unified inner and outer space, I am simultaneously allowing you to explore your own energy. Whenever I "read" you as belonging to a certain bodymind type or structure, I am respecting your capacity to break the limits of this classification and to find your own limits.

171

A number of bodyworkers and therapists have explored a wide variety of physical and psychological types. In **Know Your Type** (4) Ralph Metzner outlines and summarizes a selection of types, including those of Sheldon (mesomorph, endomorph, and ectomorph); Kurtz (bottom-heavy, top-heavy, burdened, rigid, and needy types); and Jung (introvert and extrovert). He also gives various psychiatric types from Freud, Reich, and Lowen, and the classic western types (choleric, sanguine, phlegmatic, and melancholic). Rather than a further review of these types, I offer a classification system which has evolved from my work over the years. My schema is intended to supplement and not replace the types specified by Metzner and is designed to be flexible in providing individuals with a framework which allows interaction with the practitioner.

This schema does not try to classify the individual directly but indicates that some detectable characteristics or structure may belong to a type or number of types. This gives a starting point from which the individual can be expressive, without being treated as an object. For example, instead of indicating that you are a "burdened type," I may share with you that your shoulders look heavy, and ask you how you feel in your shoulders. With this kind of shared impression and interrogation our interaction can more likely develop into a discovery of what you feel and want and what I, in turn, can give to you.

Exchange the following with a friend:

Face each other and share what you see in each other's structure. Be sure to ask if your partner feels that your impression is true. Encourage an exploration of the feeling and thoughts in various parts of the body by exaggerating the position or exploring an alternative position. Try out a type which you resemble (top-heavy, bottom-heavy, etc.) by saying, for example, both: "I am top heavy," and "I am not only top-heavy," that is, affirm that part of the classification you accept and deny what you don't accept.

We may discover in the process of interacting and sharing that what is happening in your shoulders is of less

BODYMIND TYPES

TYPE	OUTSIDE STRUCTURE, SHELL	INSIDE INTRINSIC STRUCTURE	FUNCTION	COMPARISON TO OTHER TYPES
I. EXPANDING outer directed A. SOFT	LOOSE: superficial tissue available, fat porous, voluminous; reaction is slow but responsive	United Core TIGHT: hidden, frozen, immobile	Outer sleeve is protective cushion for unused inner energy	Extrovert who hides inner feeling, bottomheavy, seductive, rigid inside, paralyzed paranoic, masochistic, burdened, endomorph
B. HARD	TIGHT: thick skinned, muscular, dense, quick voluminous, massive	LOOSE: little tone, weak, confused, underdeveloped	Strong, active exterior covers fragile inner energy	Extrovert with little inner development, topheavy, manipulative, sadist, rigid outside, mesomorph
II. CONTRACTING inner directed A. HARD	TIGHT OR LOOSE: Unconscious, unresponsive, rubbery, fronzen, stoic	DUAL CORE — Outer Core / Inner Core TIGHT — Both are underdeveloped	Lack of outside consciousness compensated by active introverted energy	Active introvert, phlegmatic outside, choleric inside, compulsive, anal, ectomorph
B. Soft	LOOSE: unconscious, unresponsive, rubbery, fronzen, stoic	TIGHT: outer core restricts inner core / LOOSE: inner core is weak and fragile	Inner activity is not well directed	Confused introvert, needy, oral, masochist, melancholic, burdened, endomorph, hysteric
III. UNSTABLE excess inside or outside A. OVEREXTENDING 1. CONTRACTING	STABLE	TIGHT: Entire Core is Overactive or TIGHT: Outer Core Traps Inner	Under stress energy is focused inside or outside for protection	Part time introvert or part time extrovert, neurotic, body changes frequently
2. EXPANDING	LOOSE: overconscious or unresponsive TIGHT: overprotective	STABLE		
B. FLUCTUATING	UNSTABLE	UNSTABLE	Unpredictable and excessive movement toward both expansion and contraction	Schizoid, manic depressive, hysteric, oscillating mixture of many types
IV. EVEN equal tone A. HARD EVEN	TIGHT	TIGHT	Even but excessive tone; too protective in both shell and core	Has capacity to be open but holds back some of energy
B. SOFT EVEN	LOOSE	LOOSE	Even but inadequate tone; too open in both shell and core	Has capacity to conserve energy, but gives away too much
C. BALANCED	OPEN TO CHANGE	BALANCED: outside and inside is even; shell and core disappear	Allows energy to flow to where it is needed	Genital, spontaneous, loving, both open and self-protective

importance to your release and integration than what is happening in other parts of your structure. We may discover that a feeling of neediness around your mouth and throat is equally significant as, or even more significant than, my initial observation about your shoulders.

Type consideration is merely a suggested starting point for discovery and transformation. After the client moves through his or her process of transformation, we can then look back and consider the degree of change and how much movement has been made away from the type with which we started. Now that there has been change, the client, for example may no longer be very much like a "needy" type, he or she may be fuller, softer, and more expanded, and more closely resemble what I presently shall describe as an "even" type. This flexible approach to types allows a discovery of limitations and a decision about what one wants to accept or work to overcome.

Jonathan was a professor of philosophy. His body was lean, small-boned and somewhat boyish and fragile, while his head was relatively large and pointed. He had been trying to gain weight for years by lifting weights and taking protein supplements, and although his muscles had tightened, he had not become much larger.

As I started working with him, I expected a softening and balancing of his body but no major changes in his size. I encouraged him to stop heavy exercise, pointing out that his body was close to what Sheldon has classified as ectomorph (thin body, large head, lack of muscular development). After I had worked with him for seven sessions, I was surprised that he looked much larger, much more expanded in his musculature; even his bones seemed to have grown.

He shared with me that during the previous week he had a flashback memory, which he felt through his whole self. He remembered that at the age of five he was unable to compete with his brothers in feats of physical strength and skill and so he had turned to mental activity in an attempt to gain the approval of his parents. Yet he still felt insecure and had started lifting weights in an attempt to prove to himself he was really powerful. After seven sessions, he realized he did not have to compete but could explore his physical strength in other ways. He began enjoying swimming, running, and dancing.

During the next six months, as I completed the remaining three sessions, he expanded two inches around his chest, and his thigh and calf muscles became full but soft. And even his head was less pointed. I was happily surprised that he went far beyond the limits I had initially envisaged for him.

Early in life we begin to develop our strength and consciousness by concentrating more on the outside or more on the inside of ourselves. In so doing we armor ourselves in characteristic ways that resemble what I call "expanding" and "contracting" types of bodymind. When we fluctuate unevenly between outside and inside, we may resemble what I call an "unstable" type. When our inner and outer rhythms are somewhat equal, we may resemble what I want to call an "even" type. Even when the range of expansion and contraction is to a certain extent restricted, we may still be close to an even type.

The following classifications evolved more from tactile than visual cues, so are difficult to illustrate, except in the accompanying cross sections of the body. They also cut across previous classifications, that is to say, one of my types may be similar to more than one traditional type. The chart provided is not complete or definitive, but I hope it suggests to you examples of such types from your own experience.

EXPANDING TYPES
Taking Up Outer Space

We have moods in which we are outgoing, in which we make contact with the people around us or the objects in our environment. In this external movement we may be enthusiastic and filled with vitality and purpose, or quiet, slow, and not so clearly directed. There are many individuals who focus the main part of their lives on this extroverted dimension and who in some ways neglect the inner side of themselves. They display a kind of expanding, well-developed outer armor or defense in dealing with life. The chart shows two possible expanding types: a soft one, which is loose outside and tight inside, and a hard one, which is tight outside and loose inside.

The first kind of expanding person has developed a loose outer sleeve around the body (mind), providing a soft, fat, porous protection for absorbing the pains, demands, shocks, and tensions of everyday life. Although this large, elastic surface creates a broad, flexible contact with the world and other people, it is a shell, a kind of cushion, allowing the individual to react from the outside, perhaps slowly, without expressing the more contracted inner feelings. The inside remains frozen and mostly unconscious, used only when the individual is touched deeply, or when called upon to use his or her reserve strength. Whenever I am working with a person whose tissue and personality show some of these traits, I explore the direction of our work together by either provoking the person outside, encouraging a quicker response to me, or by trying to work my way slowly through the soft, outer shell to the evasive deepest tissue, feelings, and thoughts.

Maria, from Florence, had been married to her domineering husband ten years. She was obedient to him, but was not at all timid, and managed to go around him when she really wanted something to which he was opposed. She was not very fat but rather large in the hips and upper thighs. Her tissue was spongy and rubbery and she had little

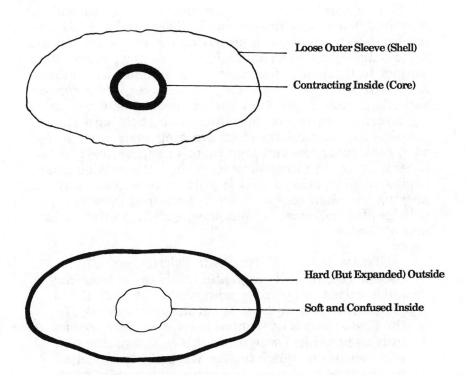

The first kind of expanding person develops a loose outer sleeve around the body(mind), providing a soft, fat or porous protection, a cushion against pain and tension. The second kind of expanding type is muscular, massive, dense, or thick- skinned and can withstand a great deal of outer stress.

feeling on the surface and at the intermediate level of tissue. As I worked I had to hook the tissue sharply with my fingers, take up any slack, and hold my grip encouraging her to breathe more rapidly and to make loud sounds as she exhaled. Gradually, with each session, she began to respond faster, and to understand that it was o.k. for her to let her deeper feelings come to the surface.

The second kind of expanding type is muscular, massive, dense, or thick-skinned. These individuals also use their body volume as a protection device. Since they are tight outside, they can take, and even enjoy, more rough contact to the point of aggressive interaction with others. Although their reactions may be quicker, they remain superficial unless the hard shell is broken or dissolved. I try forceful, aggressive encounter with such hard shelled individuals, or else I try circumventing their outer armor with gentleness, encouraging them to expose their looser, inner selves. In either strategy, when the outside armor begins to disappear, I find it helpful to explore ways of keeping the often confused, underdeveloped interior intact with guided movements, and slow, careful initiation into new attitudes.

Tony was an English "skin head." He considered himself tough and ready to confront the authorities or rowdies who were not part of his gang. Underneath he was actually very needy. In the first sessions he wanted to express his anger as fully as possible. I supported this by provoking him with words and quick taps on the belly, but I waited for the moment he would accept more gentle work. During the fourth session after he had exploded with anger and was trembling in exhaustion, I rocked him softly and sang a lullaby. As he began sobbing I was able, without much pressure, to begin moving through previously resistant layers of tissue.

You can look at yourself in relation to the expanding types with the following:

Do you consider yourself to be ample and soft on the outside of your body? Can you easily grasp the flesh of your thighs between your thumb and forefinger? When you squeeze hard to you feel any pain? Consider whether you have a rather soft and unconscious protective buffer on the outside of your body. If you see yourself as soft and expanding, do yo also see that at a deeper level you have a lot of resistance?

Do you think of yourself as rather large and tight on the surface? Is it difficult to pinch the flesh on your thighs? Do you like a lot of vigorous activities like running, swimming, dancing? Did you fight or wrestle with other children when you were a child? If you consider yourself as hard and expanding, reflect on whether you are clear about your inner feelings, and whether you find it easy to be alone, to meditate quietly.

CONTRACTING TYPES
Busy Inner Worlds

Whereas the life of the expanding type is filled with outer contact, the contracting individual withdraws and holds back from external engagement and interaction. These individuals perhaps appear calm on the surface, but underneath create conscious, active, and tense inner movements (which contrasts with the frozen inactivity of the soft, expanding type who is also tight inside).

This inner activity takes two forms. First in the hard, contracting type, the entire core structure is overactive and the shell neglected, as in the case of the person who is continually avoiding any outer contact by a frenzy of innner movement. Here the outside may be relatively loose but lacking in the receptivity of the slow, conscious responsiveness of the soft expanding type.

Second, the soft contracting type has a contraction of the deep extrinsic muscles (which we can classify as the

CONTRACTING TYPES

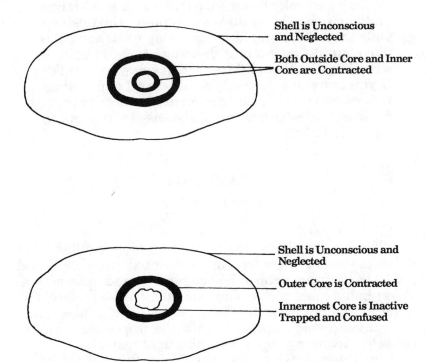

Shell is Unconscious
and Neglected

Both Outside Core and Inner
Core are Contracted

Shell is Unconscious and
Neglected

Outer Core is Contracted

Innermost Core is Inactive
Trapped and Confused

The contracting type person may be calm and soft on the surface, but underneath there is a core of activity and tense inner movement which takes two forms: 1) the entire core is overactive; 2) the peripheral part of the core traps the deep, weak, and confused muscles of the inner core.

periphery of the core), surrounding the even deeper intrinsic muscles (the inner core). The contraction of the relatively deep extrinsic muscles (peripheral core) traps the deeper intrinsic muscles (inner core) and restricts their mobility and power. (We saw in previous chapters how the psoas can be overpowered by surrounding structures). The outer core is, then, tight and over-developed, while the inner core is loose, inactive, and weak. This soft contracting type differs from the hard expanding type (who is also loose inside) in that in this type the shell is loose and relatively lacking in energetic response.

With both contracting types I encourage exploration and use of their external power -- the expression of anger, joy, enthusiasm, the open display of thoughts and feelings. With the second type, however, since the inner and outer extremes are weak (the shell and inner core are soft), I suggest that their outer movements and expressions be slow and careful explorations, accompanied by subtle, conscious inner attitudes.

First an example of a hard contracting type:

Sagarito was a religious devotee who meditated twice a day. He was always disciplining his thoughts and feelings, seeking purity and enlightenment. He felt that his body was only a vehicle to be used to help advance his spiritual aspirations. The outside of his body, although not hard like a hard expanding type, was rather lifeless. He was quiet and responsive as I pressed through the outer layers, then as I reached deeper he would stop me, saying he found that there were overwhelming images and sensations which he could not assimilate. I found the most effective way to work with him was to keep my hands at an intermediate depth, and invite him to decide when I was to go deeper. As I waited for his acceptance, I encouraged him not only to verbally express his images and feelings, but also to translate these into movements in his legs, arms, and head.

Here's an example of a soft contracting type:

Sorgen was a Danish economic professor in Copenhagen. He was rather soft on the surface and was very sincere and interested in others. But he had a theory about everybody he met and was continually intervening in other people's disputes, interpreting their attitudes toward each other. He stayed busy with these ideas, but when pressed, found it difficult to express any feelings of his own -- he would become confused if not allowed to talk about others.

In the later sessions of work, as I began waking up his deep intrinsic muscles, I encouraged him not to think or verbally express himself, but to pantomime in slow-motion his attitude toward his father, mother, and toward himself. These slow movements with exaggerated facial expressions helped him begin to focus on very concrete, simple feelings inside himself.

Find your relation to contracting types with the following:

Do you feel tight in the center of your body? Do you spend a lot of your time making decisions, fantasizing, or just thinking things over? Are you so busy that you sometimes do not notice that you have bruised or cut yourself? As a test of whether you are a hard contracting type consider whether you can totally relax, both outside and inside.

Do you keep your mind occupied, so that you won't have time to get upset? Do you use a soft, pleasant even accomodating attitude toward others to cover up your doubts and inner confusions? Do these uncertainties take a lot of your energy? If you feel that you, at least in part, fit the soft contracting type, notice how difficult it may be to make a simple decision and to carry it out, without delay or problems.

UNSTABLE TYPES
Over The Edge And Swinging Back And Forth

Some individuals easily change the direction of their energy and awareness between inside and outside so that they are not stuck in either, yet make these changes as a result of their instability and not in harmony with their needs and environment. There are two kinds of instability. One results from overextension of the self, and the other from disruptive fluctuation within the self.

Overextension is toward expansion or toward contraction. These individuals may be usually balanced in their outer and inner activity, but under stress, they focus too much of their energy either outward or inward. They may have no problem with one half of their lives. If they sometimes exhaust themselves in expanding, they may not have a corresponding degree in contracting, and though inclined to withdraw into themselves, they may still manage to cope with outside demands. Their weakness is in one direction, and unlike the previous expanding and contracting types, they can eventually, even if temporarily, regain a balance between inside and outside.

Georgia seemed like a lady who successfully handled her life. She had graduated from college and had a good paying job as a junior executive in a large firm. She was outgoing, pleasant, and efficient. But after six months of marriage her world fell apart. Her life had been built around control and discipline, but she was unable to control her husband the way she had controlled her life. She became very nervous, unsure of herself, and withdrawn.

The second kind of instability is seen in the individual who, perhaps wildly, fluctuates between extremes. These persons are unpredictably expanding in one moment and contracting in the next. Typical would be the person who

183

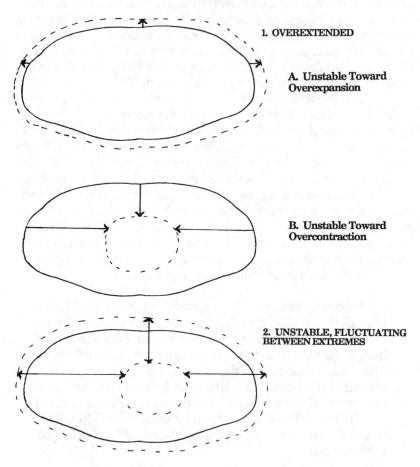

UNSTABLE TYPES

1. OVEREXTENDED

A. Unstable Toward
Overexpansion

B. Unstable Toward
Overcontraction

2. UNSTABLE, FLUCTUATING
BETWEEN EXTREMES

Unstable type persons either overextend themselves or fluctuate between extremes. They overextend their energy by contracting and restricting themselves or by expanding and using up their energy. They unpredictably fluctuate by moving from one extreme to the other of expansion.

184

gains excessive weight in a matter of days or weeks, and loses it just as quickly. This could be the manic-depressive, now joyful and overflowing, and then suddenly gravely depressed. We all expand and contract. However, depending upon the extent we are balanced and flowing, we exercise a centered and spontaneous choice about the timing, degree, and rate of our expansions and contractions.

Whenever Tim was encouraged to express himself, he fell silent and withdrew his energy. Whenever anyone tried to calm him, he became more nervous and active. Sometimes when I worked with him I could press deep into his tissue without him reacting, and then suddenly without warning he would contract and jerk away.

Both unstable types show an unevenness in tissue and attitudes. They may collapse under pressure, into a slack, disorganized state. Or if they are touched deeply, they may pull together in an overcontracting defense. In consideration of these fragilities, I have found it important to work with these individuals in a nonprovocative and predictable manner, helping them learn that change can be safe, gradual, and progressive.

Compare yourself to these unstable types with the following:

Do you find that your body is strong and stable for months at a time, and then suddenly you find yourself weak and collapsing? Are you a quiet, withdrawn person who surprises everybody by becoming the outgoing life of the party? Do you consider yourself unstable because you overextend yourself?

Do you sometimes think that you have radically different personalities which you can't control? Do you feel that there is no real you, but just different roles you play? Do the proportions of your body change enough for you to consider yourself to be in some respects an unstable fluctuating type?

EVEN TYPES
Staying Consistent And Flexible

There exist those rare individuals who balance their expanding and contracting sides, their outer and inner selves, and who change with their enviroment, but not because of it. They have bodyminds whose outer, intermediate, and deepest layers are all more or less equal in tonus, flexibility, and responsiveness. Their bodyminds have little in the way of a protective core and shell, since they are able to mobilize their entire selves when threatened from within or without. As previously stated in Chapter II:

> **When we are really alive, the core and shell disintegrate; our energy moves easily from outside to inside and from inside to outside. There is a balance between the larger extrinsic muscles which give power to our movements and the inner intrinsic muscles, which give subtle direction and stability.**

When subjected to severe stress for long periods of time, even types may tend to protect themselves, by equally restricting the range of both expansion and contraction, but not by losing their balance between inside and outside. I find them most satisfying to work with, since their transformations are rapid and smooth. Compare this kind of balanced change with the changes of expanding types, who are slow in responding to probes into their soft buffer or who melt in confusion as their hard exterior breaks open; or with the changes of contracting types, who stubbornly resist deep, gentle surrender; and with the uneven types who keep changing directions to avoid confrontation.

Hassad was a Lebanese businessman who often visited Europe. He was sanguine and friendly and had a well-proportioned body whose tissues were

EVEN TYPES

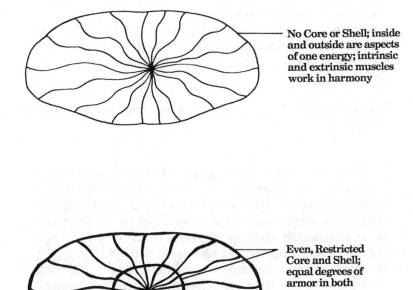

No Core or Shell; inside
and outside are aspects
of one energy; intrinsic
and extrinsic muscles
work in harmony

Even, Restricted
Core and Shell;
equal degrees of
armor in both

There exist those rare individuals who have little in the way of a protective core and shell. They are even from outside to inside, and show flexibility and balance in expanding and contracting their energy. When these even types are exposed to prolonged stress, they may also develop tension, but it is evenly distributed throughout their inner and outer structures.

187

soft, yet responsive from the outside to even the deepest layers. I had, over a period of a year, given him more than ten sessions of work on his visits to Paris. At about this time the Lebanese civil war worsened, and on his next visit I found him tight and afraid for the safety of his family.

At this point it took only one sesion to soften and balance his body. He cried a lot and expressed his anger against the war. He himself wanted to leave Lebanon but his large family wanted to stay, and he had made the decision to stay with them.

When I met him again six months later in Paris, he was again contracted and afraid. But again was able to let go quickly and express his feelings.

You can get a feeling for the even type by considering the following:

Reflect on a time in your life when you were happy for an extended period of time. Remember how you were able to ride out your difficulties without losing your sense of well-being. Remember how you were able to express different feelings freely, even anger and sadness, without getting stuck in them. Remember the health and resilience of your body, how sickness was a temporary cleansing of the body. Compare this happy period with a period in which you were blocked and unhappy.

In working with each individual, I recognize that a type is a sterotype, and that we are only looking for starting and comparison points. Each person will respond differently to the above suggested ways of exploring and working with different types. The same individual may even react differently at different times. That is why I keep making new suggestions, posing new questions, trying to discover new ways of making contact with each individual and in the process find that I am changing myself.

FOOTNOTES FOR CHAPTER VI

1. **The Myth of Mental Illness** (New York: Harper and Row, 1974) **Sex by Presciption,** Thomas Szasz (New York: Anchor, 1980).
2. **Ron Kurtz Method of Body Centered Psychotherapy, Training Manual,** Ron Kurtz (Putnam: Hakomi Institute, 1981) p. 39.
3. **Ibid.,** p.41.
4. **Know Your Type,** op. cit.

BIBLIOGRAPHY

Boadella, David, **Wilhelm Reich**. New York: Dell, 1975.

Common Ground, Resources for Personal Transformation. San Francisco: Summer 1984.

Dychwald, Ken, **Bodymind**. New York: Jove Books, 1977.

Feldenkrais, M., **The Body and Mature Behavior**. New York: International Universities Press, 1973.

Gardner, Howard, "How the Split Brain Gets a Joke," **Psychology Today**, Feb. 81.

Heckler, Richard Strozzi, **The Anatomy of Change**. Boulder: Shambhala,1984.

Johnson, Don, **The Protean Body**. New York: Harper and Row, 1974.

Keen, Sam, **Voices and Visions**. New York: Harper and Row, 1974.

Kurtz, Ronald and Hector Prestera, **The Body Reveals**. New York: Harper and Row, 1976.

Kurtz, Ron, **Ron Kurtz Method of Body Centered Psychotherapy, Training Manual**. Putnam: Hakomi Institute, 1981.

Laing, R.D., **Knots**. Middlesex: Penguin, 1970.

Lodes, Hiltrud, **Atme Richtig**. Munich: Ehrenwirth, 1977.

Lowen, Alexander, **The Physical Dynamics of Character Structure**. New York: 1958.

Mann, W.E., **Orgone, Reich, and Eros**. New York: Simon and Schuster, 1973.

Melzack, Ronald, **The Puzzle of Pain**. New York: Basic Books, 1973.

Metzner, Ralph, **Know Your Type**. New York: Anchor, 1979.

Naslednikow, Mitzu, **Le chemin de l'extase**. Paris: Albin Michele, 1981.

Ray, Sondra and Leonard Orr, **Rebirthing in the New Age**. Milbrae: Celestial Arts, 1976.

Reich, Wilhelm, **Character Analysis**. London: Vision Press, 1950.

_____, **The Function of the Orgasm**. New York: Noonday Press, 1942.

Rolf, Ida, **Rolfing, The Integration of Human Structures**. Santa Monica: Dennis Landman, 1977.

_____, "Structural Integration: A Contribution to the Understanding of Stress." **Confina Psychiatrica**, XVI (1973.

Szasz, Thomas, **The Myth of Mental Illness**. New York: Harper and Row, 1974.

_____, **Sex by Prescription**. New York: Anchor, 1980.

Todd, Mary E., **The Thinking Body**. New York: Dance Horizons, 1937.

INDEX

TRAINING CENTERS
IN ENGLISH SPEAKING COUNTRIES

UNITED STATES

The international Center for Release and Integration is located near San Francisco (mailing address: Jack Painter, 450 Hillside Avenue, Mill Valley, CA 94941; Tel. 415-383-4017). Information about training programs and certified practitioners is available. The following centers also give trainings and can recommend practitioners.

COLORADO
Janis MacKeigan, 1070 Union St., Boulder, CO 80304, Tel. 303 442-3936.

FLORIDA
Joyce Johnson, Florida Institute of Psychophysical Integration, 5837 Mariner Drive, Tampa, FL 33609, Tel. 813 286-2273.

LOS ANGELOS
Jack Haer, PhD. and Marvin Treiger, PhD., Bodymind Institute, 11061 Missouri Avenue, #4, L.A., CA 90025, Tel 213 473-3855.

MARYLAND
Donna Dryer, M.D. and Richard Yenson, PhD., Orenda Institute, 2403 Talbot Rd., Baltimore, MD 21216, 301 664-2454

MASSACHUSETTS
Samvedam, 11 Center Street, Watertown, MA 02172, Tel. 314 772-8848.

NEW MEXICO
Donald Van Hooten, 613 Kathryn Ave., Santa Fe, NM 87501, Tel. 505 988-2627.

NEW YORK
Todd Winant, 522 Shore Rd., #35, Longbeach, NY 11561, Tel. 516 431-8642.

CANADA
(Enflight and French)

Bruno Chretien, 6225 Beaubien, Montreal, HIM 3E6, Tel. 514 257-0237.

ENGLAND

Silke Ziehl, 14 Glamorgan Rd., Hampton Wick, Kingston Upon Thames, Surrey, KT1 4HP, Tel. 019772226.

Freda Copley, 2 Woodvale Terr, Hawksworth Rd., Horsforth, Leeds, LS184JW, Tel. 0532-583443.

Sean Doherty, 465 Queen's Rd., Sheffield S240R, Tel. (0742) 558165.

Susan Sidery, Old Schoolhouse, Dunkeswell Abbey, Honiton, Devon (Hemycock), Ex140RP, Tel. 0823-680537.

AUSTRALIA

Deva Daricha, Greenwood Lane Centre, Box 233, Yarra Glen, Victoria 3775.

CENTERS IN COUNTRIES WITH OTHER LANGUAGES

Contact Mill Valley for centers or practitioners in France, Germany, Sweden, Denmark, Italy, Quebec, Canada, Mexico, Brazil, and Venezuela.

Jack Painter, second from the right, is shown with a group of Postural Integrators. He is director of The International Center for Release and Integration in Mill Valley (near San Francisco) which offers training and certification in Postural Integration, Reichian Release, Rebirthing, and Pelvic-Sexual Release. He received his Ph.D. from Emory University (Atlanta) in 1961. As a Smith-Mundt scholar he pursued post-graduate research in Europe, and while serving as a professor at the University of Miami (1961-69), he also did research in physio-philosophy and psychology -- acupuncture, yoga, zazen, Reichian and Gestalt bodywork, and connective tissue manipulation. He holds a massage therapy degree from Lindsey Hopkins (Miami) and is an associate of the Instituto Wilhelm Reich in Mexico City. Since 1973 he has trained more than 1500 practitiooners of bodywork and has helped establish centers in Europe, Latin America, the U.S., and Canada.

FROM BODYMIND BOOKS

450 Hillside Avenue
Mill Valley, CA 94941
Tel. 415-383-4017

BOOKS

Technical Manual of Deep Wholistic Bodywork. A systematic outline for reorganizing the myofascia of the entire musculature; a rich synthesis of deep tissue work, breath work, emotional expression, affirmations, acupressure, and movement awareness. "Professionals of all persuasions will find much in this thorough and convincing explanation." Jack Haer, Ph.D., Director, Bodymind Inst., L.A. "Above all, this book delivers." Stuart Kutchins, O.M.D., (Doctor of Oriental Medicine). Now Available. $24.00 (includes shipping and handling)

Deep Bodywork and Personal Development, Harmonizing our bodies, Emotions, and Thoughts. A unique synthesis of deep tissue, gestalt and reichian work. Filled with technique, theory and illustrations. "A major contribution to Western psychology"-Robert Hall, M.D., (Lomi School). "Goes beyond any model I know"-Ron Kurtz(Body Reveals). For general and professional reader. $19.00 (includes shipping and handling).

Strong and Soft, Exercise for Both Physical And Emotional Health. Our Zealous training of the body can lead not only to uncomfortable tension in the body, but also to emotional rigidity. Even when we try carefully to follow the principles of body balance, our deep inner feelings subtly control and disorganize our movements. Here is a new approach to body building which encourages emotional freedom with overall bodymind strength and balance. Publication in the summer of 1990.

VIDEOS

The Power and Joy of Deep Bodywork. A close up view of how deep tissue and breathwork can change our lives. See, first hand, how being deeply touched can open hardened parts of our bodies and release long held-back or suppressed feelings. Includes an explanation, by Jack Painter, of the process of Postural Integration. Color, 30 minutes. For release in September, 1989.

Technical Review of Postural Integration for Practitioners. Precise and comprehensive review of Body Reading, Strategies, Emotional Release, Breathwork, and Manipulations, including many scenes from actual sessions. For release in September, 1989. (4 tapes) **For Practitioners Only.**

Breath and Life. Our breathing--inhalation and exhalation--is a cycle of charging and discharging energy, which we often cut short. When we do not allow our energy to build completely or to be fully expressed, we create life-long blocks. Through an explorative of the power of breathing, we can open ourselves to excitement, power , softness and love. Follow Jack Painter through many ways of breathing: chest and belly charging, panting, explosive discharging, Meditative charging and discharging, and many more. See dramatic, close-up, on-camera changes. Color, 30 minutes. For upcoming release.

Please write for upcoming books and videos.

Make checks payable to **"BODYMIND BOOKS"**.